About the Author

Charles Michael Andres Clark is Professor of Economics, Tobin College of Business and Senior Fellow, Vincentian Center for Church and Society at St. John's University, New York. His past positions include Visiting Professor, University College Cork. Professor Clark earned his Ph.D. at the New School for Social Research, writing his thesis under Robert Heilbroner's supervision. He is the author of *Economic Theory and Natural Philosophy* (1992), *Pathways to a Basic Income* (with Sean Healy) (1997) and *Basic Income: Economic Security for All Canadians* (with Sally Lerner and W. Robert Needham) (1999) and is the editor of *History and Historians of Political Economy* (1994); *Institutional Economics and the Theory of Social Value* (1995); *Unemployment in Ireland* (with Catherine Kavanagh) (1998); and *Economic Transition in Historical Perspective* (with Janina Rosicka) (2001), as well as over 70 professional publications. He lives in Long Island, New York, with his wife Lisa and their three children, Meghan Julia, Kaitlin Virginia and Charles Robert Thorstein.

The Basic Income Guarantee

Ensuring Progress and Prosperity in the 21st Century

Charles Michael Andres Clark

The Liffey Press
in association with
CORI Justice Commission

Published by
The Liffey Press
307 Clontarf Road
Dublin 3, Ireland
www.theliffeypress.com

© 2002 Charles Michael Andres Clark

A catalogue record of this book is
available from the British Library.

ISBN 1-904148-07-7

All rights reserved. No part of this publication may be
reproduced or transmitted in any form or by any means,
including photocopying and recording, without written
permission of the publisher. Such written permission must
also be obtained before any part of this publication is
stored in a retrieval system of any nature. Requests for
permission should be directed to The Liffey Press,
307 Clontarf Road, Dublin 3, Ireland.

Printed in the Republic of Ireland by Colour Books Ltd.

TABLE OF CONTENTS

Acknowledgements ....*vii*

INTRODUCTION.. 1

CHAPTER 1: Which Future Should Ireland Choose?..........11

CHAPTER 2: Ireland and the "New Economy" 23

CHAPTER 3: A Basic Income Guarantee Proposal 41

CHAPTER 4: Basic Income and Competitiveness 51

CHAPTER 5: Changing Labour Markets: Towards Real Flexibility...75

CHAPTER 6: Basic Income and Economic Progress for All 105

CHAPTER 7: Some Alternative to Our Basic Income Proposal...127

CONCLUSION: Social Justice or Blind Drift?.......................135

Bibliography..143

Acknowledgements

The research for this book was carried out under the auspices of the Conference of Religious of Ireland with the support of a research grant from the Joseph Rowntree Charitable Trust. I am greatly in the debt of Sean Healy and Brigid Reynolds for their support and encouragement on this project, as well as on many others. They set a standard of excellence in work and dedication that is truly inspirational, and near impossible to keep up with. It is my hope that this book can make a small contribution to their efforts in promoting social justice.

Numerous others have assisted in this project, which began in 1999. Many civil servants have been particularly helpful; in fact, everyone I had any contact with was extremely accommodating. Paddy Malloy of the Revenue Commissioners was especially helpful on this and earlier projects in explaining how the Revenue Commissioners estimated the tax base and with supplying updated estimates. The good folks at the Central Statistics Office also need singling out, especially those who work on the Household Budget Survey. Sean Ward, whose path-breaking work on Basic Income made all subsequent researchers' efforts considerably easier, also provided useful criticism and suggestions.

At St John's University I have had the good fortune to have a nurturing environment at the *Vincentian Center for Church and Society*, which, under the leadership of Sr Margaret John Kelly, DC and Mary Ann Dantuono, has provided an excellent atmosphere for research into how best to promote social justice.

Lastly, I have to thank my wife Lisa and my children, Meghan, Kaitlin and Chip, for keeping me sane.

INTRODUCTION

IRELAND AT A CROSSROADS

With all the changes and uncertainties that Ireland, Europe and the world currently face, it is quite fitting that we are making the transition from the second to the third millennium. Who could have predicted the past 20 or 30 years? Certainly, we knew back then that we would be facing a major change in the calendar, but a new currency? Newfound prosperity and cultural renaissance? A "new economy"? Globalisation and the Internet? Rising population and net immigration? End to the Cold War? Peace in Belfast? We live in a very different world to the one most of us were born into. Given these dramatic changes, it is quite reasonable for there to be a rethinking of other aspects of Irish society. This book addresses itself to the question of what form of social welfare system Ireland should adopt to best promote economic efficiency and social equity in the 21st century. It is natural for such a question to be raised, for a transformation in the economy always eventually causes a change in its institutions of distribution and social welfare. The old system, the post-World War II welfare state, was designed to deal with a specific type of economy and in a particular world economic environment. The context of the Irish economy (and other capitalist economies) has changed and is continuing to change, and we are far removed from the economy and society of the "golden years" of the post-war era.

The current discussions on the topic of Basic Income in Ireland, and in Europe, are a response to the changed economic environment, and it is to this conversation that this book hopes to make a contribution. There are few issues facing Ireland, and elsewhere, that are more important than how to create an economy and society in which economic progress is promoted and where all share in the benefits, and contribute to the production, of such progress. One without the other will not do. Economic efficiency without equity is political and social, and in the long run economic, suicide. Economic equity without economic efficiency will fail to meet all human needs, thus will not meet the reasonable equity criteria of a decent standard of living for all. New approaches and policies that promote both equity and efficiency, and not trade one off the other, are needed if this new century is to meet our best hopes and wishes, and not merely be a power grab by the rich and powerful and greedy. A policy of a Basic Income guarantee offers the possibility of setting the stage for a truly "great society" and Irish renaissance. In such a renaissance, Ireland's contribution to the world will not just be cultural, but will also demonstrate how to create a society and economy in which all participate and all benefit, and where no one is left behind.

What is a Basic Income?

The idea of a Basic Income guarantee is not new. The United States came very close to enacting such a system in the late 1960s and early 1970s, the legislation ultimately killed by the deep-seeded racism in the southern states (who didn't want blacks to have an independent income and thus weaken the control of elite whites over the black population). The recent rise in interest in Basic Income policies in Europe is the result, as it was in the US, of the recognition of the inherent limitations of the welfare state as a means to provide both economic security and efficiency. All of the advanced capitalist economies have been feeling these pressures since the 1970s, with some opting for more emphasis on economic growth policies based on weakening economic security commitments (US and

UK being the most outstanding examples of this trend) and others emphasising security at the expense of flexibility (the Nordic countries in particular). A Basic Income system is an attempt to provide both the flexibility necessary for a country to be competitive in the new economy as well as the level of economic security that Europeans are accustomed to and that civilised society demands.

A Basic Income system has the essential feature of a guaranteed income paid to all citizens regardless of their labour market participation. This income, which varies only according to age, is unconditional, universal and tax-free. It replaces the vast majority of public assistance programmes (except for individuals with special needs) and takes the state out of the role of regulating the poor and unemployed, as well as eliminating the stigmas that are often attached to public assistance payments. A Basic Income system could be financed in many ways, but most proposals fund them out of an income tax on all individual incomes (business income taxes remain the same), and with no exemptions, allowances or deductions. In the state of Alaska, in the US, there is a Basic Income system in the form of the Permanent Fund payments all Alaskans receive each year out of the State's oil and gas revenues. This is only a partial Basic Income system, as it does not replace any public assistance programmes, but it does show us an alternative source of funding, as well as teaching us the lesson that such a programme is very popular with the public (it is the most popular government programme in the US).

Most European countries have some universal payment programmes, typically for children and senior citizens, so the idea of an income as a right of citizenship is not new to European politics. Furthermore, all European political systems recognise the need for interventions into how the economy distributes the benefits of economic progress and activities. This is the rationale for the existence of the welfare state. A Basic Income system achieves the goal of making sure that all share in the benefits of economic progress without falling into the traps created by the welfare state and its need for active intervention in the factor markets, as well as vigorous fiscal, monetary and trade policy, in order to achieve the desired results. Such interventions are increasingly problematic in the new economy, being either undesirable or impossible.

In this book, we present an example of what a Basic Income guarantee would look like in Ireland and how it would influence both the efficiency (competitiveness) and equity (distribution of income and levels of poverty) of the Irish economy. It is of course just one example and one could come up with others that more or less fit the outline of a Basic Income policy. Creation of any actual Basic Income system in Ireland should and will be the result of the political process and the joint efforts of all four of the social pillars (government, employers, workers and the social sector). Our goal is to explore some of the economic questions and issues that are raised by any healthy public discussion on the question of Ireland changing its social welfare system.

The recent reports by the National Economic and Social Council (*Opportunities, Challenges and Capacities for Choice* 1999) and the National Competitiveness Council (*Annual Competitiveness Report* 2000), as well as numerous government reports, have reiterated Ireland's commitment to social justice, to creating an Irish society and economy in which all benefit and all participate. It is with this goal in mind that we present the analysis of this book, as it is our conclusion that a Basic Income system promotes social justice more effectively than the current system, or any other social welfare proposals currently being discussed. As social justice is our central concern, we should be very clear as to what exactly we mean by it. To this we now turn.

PROMOTING SOCIAL JUSTICE IN A 21ST CENTURY ECONOMY

The issue of social justice has been central to discussions on economics and the economy since the founding of the political economy discipline. This book is a contribution to this dialogue, with the context being the Irish economy as it enters the 21st century. Unfortunately, for much of the 20th century, most economic theorists have relegated social justice concerns to the periphery of "economics" proper, attaching the condescending label of "normative" and contrasting it with the supposedly more "scientific" designation of "positive" economics. Yet if one understands exactly what is social justice (as opposed to individual justice), then it is clear that the history of economics is the history of the striving for social justice. A vision of social justice is at the heart of the systems of thought of all the "worldly philosophers", from Adam Smith, John Stuart Mill, Karl Marx in the 18th and 19th centuries to Thorstein Veblen, John Maynard Keynes and John Kenneth Galbraith in the 20th. It is important to see Basic Income proposals in this light, for they are an attempt to promote social justice (as was the welfare state) in the new environment of globalisation and rapid technological change, what is now called the new economy.

Social justice has always had two aspects, which are mutually supporting and do not exist as a trade-off between two goals. These two aspects are: 1) the provision of sufficient resources to all members of society; 2) so that they can best contribute to their own well-being and the well-being of the community (the common good). Both reinforce each other. In order to maximise the common good, you need to have a distribution of resources such that all can participate fully in society. Gross inequality makes everyone poorer, for it limits how much is contributed to society. And in order to provide adequately for all, all must contribute. It should be apparent that social justice denies the core tenet of most policy discussions on the economy, the equity–efficiency trade-off. The central problem in the way that the equity–efficiency trade-off is used and understood by economists and policy experts is that they presuppose that equity means perfect equality (something no one advocates) and that efficiency is the maximisation of market transactions, which for practical purposes means Gross National (or Domestic) Product. Neither presupposition is ever backed up by reasonable argument or empirical evidence; it is merely assumed. Yet the conditions of social justice do not demand that the economic pie is divided equally (propounding such a criterion would be a political nightmare); nor that the output of marketable goods and services is synonymous with the common good or the well-being of the community. Differences in needs and the incentive effects for production make perfect equality not only impractical but also undesirable. Natural disasters, crime and family breakups all lead to increases in market transactions and thus in increases in the most widely used statistical measures of economic progress, GDP, but clearly they do not improve the well-being of the community. We need to rethink both equity and efficiency, defining them in such a way that the dignity of all individuals is upheld and the common good is promoted.

The challenge of social justice is, how do we create an economy in which all share in and contribute to the economic and social progress of Ireland? Creating such a society has been one of the central goals of western civilisation at least since Plato. Throughout history, social, economic and technological evolution have created the need to change *how* social justice is pursued, and the current processes of globalisation and technological transformation are prompting a needed change once again. In the agricultural economies and societies of old, social justice was promoted by ensuring that all individuals had access to sufficient land and other natural resources so that they could be productive. The majority of the rules and norms of the feudal economy centred on achieving this result (with varying degrees of success), with the Church playing the role of assisting those who fell through the cracks. With the rise of commercial society and production for the market, social justice was then promoted by insuring access to markets and eventually, with the rise of the factory system, through sufficient employment opportunities (commitment to full employment) and a just wage. The political battles of the 19th century, along with the inherent instability of capitalism, prompted the creation of the welfare state as the primary mechanism for promoting social justice. The welfare state entailed not only the provision of public assistance to those who cannot successfully compete in the marketplace, or because of a breakdown in the market system, but it also includes support for unions, labour regulation, monetary and fiscal policy, trade policy and other forms of active state intervention in the economy to promote the goals of social justice. It is the argument of this book that such methods of promoting social justice are quickly becoming ineffective and counter-productive.

We argue in Chapter 2 that the requirements of the new economy make it increasingly difficult to regulate factor markets to influence relative incomes. Add to this the effective end of fiscal and monetary policy as we know them, and we have a situation where neither equity nor social efficiency (meeting all human needs) are being achieved. If the past 300 years of economic history has taught us one economic lesson, it is that, left to themselves, markets benefit the powerful, leaving behind workers and the poor. Non-market mechanisms of distributing the benefits of economic progress to all have always been, and will always be, an essential part of all commercial societies for the simple reason that societies are more than economies, people are more than just economic actors, and "goods and services produced for the market" do not make up all that is good and serviceable in society. The economy is an evolving series of processes, and societies' methods of getting a changing economy to serve the people (rather than people serving the economy) must evolve as well.

It is because of the rise of the new economy, and the inability of the traditional welfare state to produce the results necessary to achieve social justice, that alternative social and economic policies must, and will, be discussed. It is the hope of all who are concerned with social justice that some method to lessen the disruptions and insecurities created by the new economy will take place at the early stages, that we not wait until the pain, suffering and inequities created by the new economy become so severe as to reach crisis proportions and force us to make these necessary adjustments. In the past the tendency has been to wait until the pain, dislocation and inequities created by economic transition become so severe that the survival of the society requires action. The development of the welfare state, which was an institutional adjustment necessitated by the changes brought about by the industrial revolution, after the intensified chaos and suffering caused by the Great Depression and World War II, is a good example of this. Had all the capitalist economies made these institutional adjustments when they first became necessary (late 19th century) there should be no doubt that we could have skipped both traumatic events.

PLAN OF THE BOOK

The plan of this book is quite simple. It starts off with a discussion of the values that underlie the various discussions on the future direction of the Irish economy and society. As all policy discussions are necessarily value-laden, we clearly state and discuss the values that underlie our discussion of social policy in Ireland. Our overall goal, to quote Keynes, "is to work out a social organisation which shall be as efficient as possible without offending our notions of a satisfactory way of life" (Keynes, 1963, p. 321). In Chapter 2, we discuss the context of the new economy and the changes it is bringing about and will continue to bring about. Here we use the experience of the "Great Transformation" caused by the Industrial Revolution to highlight how a change in technology and the organisation of the economy can have dramatic effects on the economy and society.

In Chapter 3, we present a hypothetical Basic Income proposal, loosely based on some that have been proposed in Ireland. In order for any discussion on the possible impact of Basic Income in Ireland to be more than just generalities, an actual system must be proposed and developed. Any actual Basic Income system will be the result of the political process and will no doubt be different in many ways. Chapter 7 provides a discussion on some alternative configurations of Basic Income systems.

Chapters 4, 5 and 6 contain the meat of the book: how a Basic Income system generally, and our Basic Income proposal specifically, will affect the competitiveness of the Irish economy, the labour market and the distribution of income and levels of poverty. These chapters are designed to meet many of the questions raised about the possible impact of a Basic Income on the Irish economy in a rigorous and empirical (where possible) manner. Each of these chapters examines the current situation in Ireland, the role of the new economy and the increased need for flexibilities it requires, and how a Basic Income system would impact on these three critical areas of the Irish economy. In the concluding chapter, we return to the goals and principles set out in Chapter 1 to evaluate our Basic Income proposal, based on the criteria stated in Chapter 1 and on the overall goal of promoting social justice in a 21st-century economy.

Chapter 1

WHICH FUTURE SHOULD IRELAND CHOOSE?

INTRODUCTION

Ireland's economic future will be determined by two factors:

1. How successfully it competes in the global economy; and
2. How it can ensure that the economic progress that comes from success in the global economy is both real and shared by all.

The first factor without the second is the Brazilianisation of Ireland; the second without the first is Euro-sclerosis. Ireland stands at a crossroads — which future will she choose?

There should be no doubt that the world economy is going through a dramatic transformation unequalled since the great transformation brought about by the Industrial Revolution. It is instructive to keep these changes in a historical context, for if we only marvel at the daily news stories on "the latest breakthrough", we will not understand the truly revolutionary nature of these developments, and we will not be able to respond with public policy adjustments and innovations that will allow *all of Ireland* to benefit from this new economy. Just as the last great transformation required a considerable amount of institutional adjustment and policy change, both to allow the march of economic progress and to ensure that the benefits of this progress are fairly and widely shared, so too will this current great transformation. As Ireland did not, for the most part, participate in the first great transformation[1] it does not have the historical memory of the changes to the economy brought about by the Industrial Revolution, and the corresponding long and painful struggle by workers and the population as a whole to create an environment in which the benefits of this new economy (industrialisation) to be shared by all (the creation of the welfare state). This could prove to be to Ireland's advantage, as the vested interests in those battles are not as entrenched as they are on the continent. As ironic as it may sound, the Irish are an ancient people in a new country and a new economy and thus have possibilities for the future that are not as open to other countries.

This book is about just these possibilities; about creating in Ireland a society which can best benefit from this "new economy" and that will ensure that *all* share in these benefits. The two key questions facing Ireland, and all the other developed countries, are: 1) how to create real economic progress in the new economy (responding to the twin issues of globalisation and technological change); and 2) how to provide the level of economic security and participation that are the hallmark of a civilised society? This is no easy task, especially since the majority of politicians and economists feel that these two goals are contradictory; you could have more of one but only by sacrificing some of the other. What is needed is an institutional framework that goes beyond this trade-off between efficiency and equality, a policy that promotes both flexibility and security. This book looks at a policy that strongly claims to do just this: the Basic Income proposal. It places this proposal in the context of the developments in the world economy and Ireland's place in this "new economy", and in the context of the values that historically have provided the underpinning of Irish society and culture. In order to ensure an Irish economy and society that fully reflects these values, it is necessary to not only fully understand the dynamics of the new economy, but to clearly state these values and goals. In this chapter, we will discuss a possible framework for creating a values-based social policy. We will do this by discussing two recent statements of the values and goals that should provide the moral principles to guide social and economic policy in Ireland: the "Eight Guiding Principles for Reform of Tax and Social Welfare System" developed by the Conference of Religious of Ireland (CORI) and the "Foundations and Principles Underpinning a Socially Inclusive Society" of the National Economic and Social Council's report *Opportunities, Challenges and Capacities for Choice*. By stating at the outset the role of values and principles in creating economic and social policy, we hope to emphasise that the central question of this study, indeed the central question facing the advanced capitalist economies, is what type of society and economy does Ireland wish to create? The future will be shaped mostly by the choices that are made, at the level of the individual, family, communities and society as a whole. In order to make rational choices, criteria of choice must be developed. Priorities need to be established, goals need to be set, and values need to be at the centre of all decision-making. Finally, it is only by clearly stating the values and principles we wish to adhere to that we can make judgements and evaluations as to which policies best promote society's goals.

CORI's EIGHT GUIDING PRINCIPLES FOR REFORM OF TAX AND SOCIAL WELFARE SYSTEM

The values and goals listed here are specific to the topic of reform of the tax and social welfare system. For a full discussion of these values and goals, see the following CORI publications: *Towards an Adequate Income for All* (1994); *An Adequate Income Guarantee for All: Desirability, Viability, Impact* (1995); *Progress, Values and Public Policy* (1996), which also extends the list to those values that should underpin measures of economic progress; *Priorities for Progress* (1999); and, most recently, Chapter Five in *Resources and Choices* (1999). In this section, I will expand on the economic significance of each of these goals and principles. Their moral, political, social and theological aspects have been developed in the above-mentioned publications.

Nature and Its Resources Are for the Benefit of All

One of the most damaging delusions of our modern individualistic culture and its corresponding "world view" is the idea that each individual somehow makes their own way in a modern economy and society. Any clear understanding of economics would show that as individuals we are poor and for the most part helpless. Very few of us ever learn the skills necessary for a self-sufficient existence, even at the most basic level of prehistoric man. We are well off because of our participation in society, and the largest contributing factor to our economic well-being is not the result of our individual efforts. It is the existence of natural resources (which are a gift from God), the inheritance of knowledge and technology (which is the sum total of all human existence over the past 40,000 years or so) and the social institutions that have been developed to organise our social and economic activities.

Society and economy are now, and have always been, a collective effort, relying on a wide range of contributions. Some of these contributions are rewarded under the current rules that guide the market economy (although very unevenly and not in proportion with actual contributions to the economy or society) while other activities are not recognised by these rules. But I think we would have a hard time finding an intelligent observer who would claim that only market contributions are important. Even Adam Smith, in *The Wealth of Nations*, noted the fundamental importance of what he called "unproductive labour", that is, labour that does not generate profits "to the master". The reality is that wealth and income are socially created and not individually created. We, as individuals, are wealthy because we live in a wealthy society and the main source of this wealth is the knowledge and social institutions that humans have developed over the centuries, which we have inherited from those who came before us, and the resources found in nature. Any contribution a specific individual makes is marginal at best. Thus there are two reasons why all should benefit from economic progress:

1. Economic output and progress is not due solely to the factors of production rewarded in market activity, but are more due to the accumulated human knowledge and natural resources, both of which are gifts from God and are only legitimately turned into private property so that they can more efficiently and effectively be used to promote the common good. Thus all have the right to a fair share of the benefits of economic progress. Anything short of this is theft.

2. In order for all to contribute to society all must have adequate resources for social participation. The marginalised and excluded are denied the possibility of contributing to society. Ensuring that all benefit means also ensuring that all can contribute.

Adequacy

The right to an adequate standard of living is a stated right in the United Nations *Declaration of Human Rights* and there are many moral and political reasons for asserting such a right. Yet there are also many economic benefits to such a right. The provision of an adequate standard of living is a minimum requirement for any level of social participation, including economic participation. People contribute to the economy in numerous ways, as producers and workers, as consumers and in establishing and promoting an environment conducive to economic prosperity. Some of these efforts are in the social economy and this activity also involves working and producing, except that it is non-market production — production that meets needs rather than wants measured in monetary terms. These efforts are essential for civil society, upon which economic society rests. Provision of an adequate standard of living is necessary if all these types of economic participation — working and producing, consumption, civic activities and participation in the social economy — are to be carried out at the levels necessary to sustain a healthy society and economy. The tendency is to argue in the other direction — that a prosperous economy is necessary in order to provide an adequate income for all — but the causality runs both ways, and high levels of inequality and poverty bring the whole economy down.

Guaranteed

Experience shows that if rights, such as the right to an adequate standard of living, are to be meaningful, they must be guaranteed for all. There are economic arguments for this as well. Economic insecurity is a real cost to society and to individuals, reducing output and consuming real resources. Reducing economic insecurity will make the economy more efficient. If society adopts the view that all should have an adequate standard of living, then the only way this can be achieved for certain is to have it guaranteed by statute. The placing of restrictions, establishing who is "deserving", weakens the commitment of "All to All". Furthermore, it leads to the needless waste of economic resources (labour, capital and land) to the regulation of those deemed to be the undeserving poor, or for establishing and regulating the deserving poor. Such regulation stigmatises the poor and makes it more difficult for them to enter the paid workforce or other forms of social participation.

Eliminate Poverty Traps

As stated above, efforts to regulate the poor often create poverty traps, a system of incentives that become a barrier for the poor to move out of poverty. Some of these incentives come from the tax and social welfare system, and it must be mentioned that the government has worked to eliminate many of these that existed in the tax code.

Equity

Equity deals with the fairness of the tax and social welfare system. Typically, economists consider vertical and horizontal equity as a goal, yet both are essential aspects of the perceived fairness of the system, a perception that has a considerable impact on the economic behaviour of citizens. Perceived unfairness leads to much inefficiency through its distortion of economic behaviour. It also increases the transaction costs of many types of economic activity, not the least being the financing of public goods and government expenditures.

Efficiency

Although all would agree that a tax and social welfare system should be efficient, defining what is "efficiency" is no easy task. Most often, economists have fallen back on the use of solely monetary measures, such as gross domestic product or personal income, or other economic categories. For the purpose of this study, efficiency is concerned with the improvement of the socio-economic situation of the whole country, with an emphasis on maximising social participation in all its forms.

Simplicity and Transparency

One of the goals of a social welfare system is to promote social cohesion. The perception, whether real or not, that such a system favours one group over another, acts like a cancer on social cohesion. The only way to combat this is to make the social welfare system simple and transparent so that everyone understands it and can see that all are being treated equitably and fairly.

Reduce Dependency

An essential goal of human flourishing and social participation is individual autonomy. This does not mean that individuals can or will live on their own, separate from society, but that they will have as much control and influence over their lives as possible. A social welfare system should aim to reduce all forms of dependency and increase autonomy. It should give people from all backgrounds the incentive to study and increase their skill levels so that they can participate more fully in the life of the community, and in the ways they feel are best for them and the community.

FOUNDATIONS AND PRINCIPLES UNDERPINNING A SOCIALLY INCLUSIVE SOCIETY

The role which values and "vision" plays in discussions of social policy in Ireland is best exemplified in the report issued by the National Economic and Social Council, titled *Opportunities, Challenges and Capacities for Choice* (1999). In this pivotal statement on the decisions Ireland needs to make to construct a society and economy adapted to the realities of the new economy and which fits Ireland's values, the report not only clearly states the "key objectives" of social policy (i.e. the goals), it also goes to some length to explain the underlying principles from which these goals are derived. The objectives mentioned in the NESC report stress economic and social inclusion; adaptation to change; and sustainability — all objectives that our Basic Income proposal attempts to meet (we will return to this in the last chapter). Furthermore, the NESC report also includes the "Foundations and Principles Underpinning a Socially Inclusive Society", listing the various international conventions and charters Ireland has been party to that make such commitments, as well as domestic agreements (such as Partnership 2000). These "foundations" stress the importance of social equality as a vital underpinning of public policy.

The stated values of the NESC report are described below.

Social Equality

Social equality underpins public policy and is a recognition of the fundamental rights of all citizens. These rights are spelled out and elaborated in various international covenants and agreements, including the United Nations *Declaration of Human Rights*, and is a fundamental value underpinning the European Union. *Partnership 2000* had numerous provisions to promote and protect social equality.

Social Inclusion

"Social inclusion[2] is essentially about full participation in society and such participation is dependent on access to citizenship rights and the exercise of citizenship responsibilities. . . . [C]itizenship rights and obligations . . . include not only the widely taken for granted civil and political rights and obligations but also social, economic and cultural rights that guarantee equality of opportunity and access to education, employment, health, housing and social services. The associated citizenship obligations include the payment of taxes and the fulfilment of the requirements implied by access to services and benefits" (NESC, 1999, pp. 76–7).

Social Partnership

Social partnership has many forms, the most obvious being the various national forums and agreements, yet here NESC is promoting the idea of a "social partnership ethos in the public policy area" (p. 79). NESC states that "it would be a mistake to conceive social partnership narrowly as what happens in the negotiation of centralised agreements or to assume that there is one perfect model of partnership agreement at the national level or only one national–local level balance. Instead, we should consider what actions are needed to secure the foundations of partnership structures broadly conceived" (p. 81).

Sustainability

The NESC report calls for development that is "sustainable economically, socially and environmentally", concentrating on "adjustments to economic integration and tackling key societal imbalances and enhancing social inclusion". One of the significant factors discussed under the heading of sustainability is the important role of the community and voluntary sectors and the role they play in social partnership.

The stated goals (objectives) of the NESC report are described below.

Economic Inclusiveness through Full Employment

"A full-employment[3] society means full employment based on a high employment/population ratio and high labour force participation of men and women and the absence of long-term unemployment." Included is a commitment to provide a "support structure that facilitates employment and/or education for those with caring responsibilities" (p. 50).[4]

Adaptability, Full Development of Information Society, Lifelong Learning

The key of adaptability is a labour force that is flexible, thus improving competitiveness. The emphasis on lifelong learning and full development of the information society is how this adaptability is to be achieved.

Sustainable and Balanced Regional Development

This goal is an expression of the value of sustainability, emphasising the balance between regional and urban development.

Further Development of the European Union

Much of Ireland's recent economic success is attributed to its participation in the European Union; thus, promoting more linkages is an important goal.

Entrepreneurial Culture

"An entrepreneurial culture implies a climate of development that values creativity, innovation, risk-taking and initiative. The fostering of an entrepreneurial culture is essential for the development of new enterprises, the growth of SMEs and an expansion in related employment" (p. 61). The development of an "entrepreneurial culture" aims to reduce Ireland's dependence on foreign firms and investment.

Supporting Work, Family and Community in the "New Economy"

It is unrealistic to think that such dramatic changes in the economy as those being generated by globalisation and technological change will have only economic benefits and no economic or social costs. As the institutions of the labour market change to provide the needed flexibilities of the new economy, new ways must be found to support the foundational institutions of society, the family and communities. We need to remember that every market requires a social context to support it and allow it to function, and that this will be as true for the economic institutions of the new economy as it has been true for all other phases of capitalist development. The new economy places even greater stress on families and social relationships, as well as greatly increasing the role of education and training, both of which become lifelong processes. New public policies to support the family and communities must therefore be implemented.

In any discussion of the values and goals of social policy, we should keep a clear idea of the difference between means and ends. The end of social policy, in fact the end of the economy, should be human flourishing, allowing individuals to maximise their potential and social participation in terms that they set. The economy is for the people, and not the reverse. Economies, and social policy, are means towards this end. The perspective of many is to look at the economy as the end and, in effect, they promote policies that force people to serve the economy. To quote Robert Heilbroner, "the market is a good servant but a horrible master". If the goals of full employment and labour market flexibility are seen as ends in themselves instead of as the means to an end, we will wind up following policies that will lower the quality of life, weaken social institutions and families and eventually destroy the economic prosperity we were striving for. It should be remembered that Mexico has the lowest level of unemployment in the Organisation for Economic Co-operation and Development (OECD) over the past 20 years (because they have no support for the unemployed) and that David Ricardo's "iron law of wages" could also be implemented to achieve labour market balance.[5]

The great challenge of the 21st-century economy is to promote real efficiency and equity not only to ensure future progress, but also to ensure that all get to benefit from this progress. This is the goal of Basic Income proposals — to use the benefits created by the new economy to create an Ireland in which all participate to their fullest potential.

Endnotes

[1] For a variety of reasons, all stemming from Ireland's status as an English colony.

[2] Social inclusion is listed as both a value and a goal.

[3] What exactly constitutes full employment is a controversial issue in economics. Traditionally, it meant that all who desired a job could find one (or more technically, the number of job vacancies was equal to the number of job seekers). In the 1970s and 1980s, the idea of a natural rate of unemployment was developed so as to legitimate the high unemployment rates in OECD countries and justify government inaction. This idea has very weak (and dubious) empirical foundations and has now been dropped by the majority of economic policy analysts. To promote social well-being, full employment must be based on choice. The goal of society should be to maximise social participation, which directly determines individual well-being and happiness, and allow the individual to choose the form of social participation.

[4] This attempt to force an increase in the labour participation rates of those with "caring responsibility" (read: those in the social and voluntary economy and especially parents engaged in child care) should be openly discussed. Evidence from America shows that this is achieved by reducing the real wages of male heads of households, thus forcing mothers of young children to work to prevent a decline in the family standard of living. The benefits of such a policy fall solely to the employers, who get a larger labour force at lower wages, while the majority of those who are "encouraged" to undertake both paid employment along with their "caring responsibilities" are made to work many more hours and have greatly increased stress levels, not to mention the social costs which include increases in crime, juvenile delinquency and added health costs.

[5] Labour markets in Ricardo's model were brought into balance (equilibrium) through adjustments in the supply of labour caused by increases and decreases in mortality rates.

Chapter 2

IRELAND AND THE "NEW ECONOMY"

THE CURRENT "GREAT TRANSFORMATION"

Few can now doubt that the economies of the world are going through a period of rapid change and transformation. Whether this is a "new economy" or merely an acceleration of the evolutionary trends of the past 200 years is a question for academics to debate. What is beyond debate is that many of our old assumptions and beliefs about the economy and the institutions and relations that determine economic outcomes no longer hold. In many ways we are at a turning point in economic history not unlike the one Karl Polanyi wrote about in his classic *The Great Transformation* (1944). This book is particularly helpful in trying to understand the current situation, because it highlights the fact that economic transformations do not happen in a vacuum and that they are not neutral in their impact on the various individuals that make up society. Three points that Polanyi emphasised are worth keeping in mind when considering the current transformation. First, technological change requires institutional change; that is, society must change the "rules and habits" by which the economy and society is organised. Second, institutional changes generated by the economy will shift the costs of the new production methods to those with the least power and influence, the poor and workers. Third, and finally, these changes will generate a social backlash by those adversely affected by the new economic order. An examination of the effects of the industrial revolution on Britain (and elsewhere) illustrates these points. The development of the factory system not only replaced the old production units, it changed society completely. This change was not a mere change in the goods and services produced, or in the methods of production. Political systems changed, social values and units changed; in fact, just about all aspects of society were recreated to fit the new order. These changes created great hardship on those who had the least ability to protect themselves from these changes: the poor, workers, women and children. These facts are all well known and are part of our cultural memory and literary heritage (Dickens being the most famous example). And these hardships generated a reaction that culminated in the creation of the welfare state.

It should be remembered that the welfare state was an institutional response to the changes (economic, political and social) created by the industrial revolution, and makes no sense in a society before the industrial revolution. The industrial revolution required the break-up of the traditional self-sufficient extended family units, eliminating the various forms of social and economic security that had previously existed. It also created the means by which life expectancy could be increased, thus increasing the demand for a system of providing for the elderly just as the traditional systems of support were being eroded. This is true of all the various sub-populations for which the welfare state provides protection: children (who first needed protection from the factory system, and who eventually needed a system of support while they raised their human capital to the levels necessary for the technologically advancing production systems); the unemployed (the economy needed a more flexible labour force, not to mention the benefits to the employers of the industrial reserve army); and those who could not compete successfully in the emerging market economy (for an endless list of reasons). The various institutions that make up the welfare state were designed to complement the economy of the mid- to late 20th century. They are based on a set of assumptions that held for the post-World War II economy, but that are no longer fully applicable.

WHY 20TH-CENTURY ECONOMIC INSTITUTIONS DO NOT FIT THE 21ST-CENTURY ECONOMY

One of the reasons that the post-WWII period was the "golden age" of capitalism is that its social and political institutions underwent a dramatic change to complement the advances in economics and technology. The creation of the welfare state played a key role in this economic progress, because it helped to spread the benefits of economic progress to all, or at least to most. These efforts at inclusion were necessary not only for the generation of economic progress, but also because they allowed for stronger democratic institutions and for a more civil society. The model used for structuring the economy so that all or most of the citizens shared in the benefits of economic progress has been called (at least in the English-speaking countries) the Keynes-Beveridge model. This model was set up under the following assumptions:

1. **Full employment as the norm.** The experience of the wartime economies showed that Keynes's policy suggestions worked and that full employment could be achieved. If there were bouts of unemployment, they would be temporary and short-lived. Keynesian fiscal and monetary policy would keep the economy at or near full employment.

2. **Productivity gains were passed on to workers**. Various institutions were set up to ensure that the gains of economic progress would be widely shared. Most of these involved intervention in various labour markets with labour unions, workplace regulations, minimum wages, subsidised benefits such as health care and retirement pensions, and a progressive tax system that checked the growth of income inequality.

3. **One worker per household**. Under the Keynes-Beveridge model, each household should be able to have a standard of living within the accepted norms of a decent quality of life provided one of the household's adults participated full-time in the labour force.

4. **Rising Real Wages.** Wage increases that reflected productivity gains allowed for rising standards of living, while also supporting non-market contributions to the economic and social life of the community and household.

In order to pursue such a model, both macro and micro policies must be used.

- **Necessary Macroeconomic Policies included**: fiscal policies (the ability to raise and lower taxes and spending levels, including deficit spending, in order to regulate aggregate demand); monetary policy (ability to raise or lower interest rates to counter inflation and influence aggregate demand); and trade policy (use of trade barriers to protect home production and the use of trade surpluses to generate aggregate demand and use imports to fight inflation, and, after 1971, the ability to manipulate one's currency to influence trade and inflation).

- **Necessary Microeconomic Policies included**: price regulation; investment subsidies; minimum wages and other wage regulations; labour regulations (on all aspects of work and remuneration); intervention in capital, land and resource factor markets; and the use of taxes and subsidies to promote greater levels of income equality, and income supports for those who, for whatever reason, could not compete successfully in the market economy. (In many countries there were strict demarcations between those who had legitimate reasons for their lack of success in the market economy, such as age, illness, unemployment, and those who did not. This is the Elizabethan demarcation between the deserving and non-deserving poor.)

It is only with these assumptions and complementary macro and microeconomic policies that the welfare state was able to ensure that all or most of society was able to share in the economic progress of the post-WWII era. Starting at the beginning of the 1970s, however, these conditions started to falter, and the welfare state economies started to come under increasing strain. The first and second oil shocks dramatically reduced the aggregate demand for the goods and services that these economies produced. The extra revenues that went to pay for the increasingly higher energy cost meant reductions in money being spent on domestically produced goods and services, which translates into higher unemployment rates. Furthermore, the higher energy costs led to inflation. Thus you had the infamous *stagflation*, rising prices *and* unemployment levels. The rising unemployment levels prevented the use of Keynesian fiscal policies to fight inflation (tax increases), as aggregate demand was already insufficient. Thus a monetary policy of high interest rates was used to fight inflation. This had an even greater dampening effect on aggregate demand, and by the end of the 1970s and early 1980s, many countries had double-digit levels of unemployment.

Unemployment

The rise in unemployment in Europe can be seen clearly in Figure 2.1, which shows the general fall in unemployment rates throughout the 1950s followed by low levels in the 1960s and a trend upward since the 1970s.

Here we see dramatic reductions in unemployment rates as Europe rebuilds itself after WWII, and by the early 1960s full employment has been reached. This low level of unemployment is maintained until the early 1970s, following the first oil price shock, and then the rate of unemployment in all European countries trends upward.

The unemployment problem became so intractable that many economists started to theorise that there was a level of unemployment that the economy could not get below, a natural rate of unemployment. Furthermore, these economists suggested that this natural rate had risen, with estimates of this so-called natural rate for the US going as high as 7 per cent. The "natural rate of unemployment" theory has turned out to be both theoretically and empirically weak, as a few countries (US, The Netherlands) have unemployment rates well below their estimated "natural rate" with no real signs of inflation. However, the countries that have significantly lowered their unemployment rates in the 1990s (US, Ireland, UK, The Netherlands) have done this without the generalised prosperity of all OECD or European economies (which was the case in the 1960s). Ireland, as we will see later in this book, has done this with high levels of foreign capital (which historically has been very fickle) and large foreign trade surplus (exporting unemployment).

Figure 2.1: Unemployment Rates, 1950–88 (selected countries)

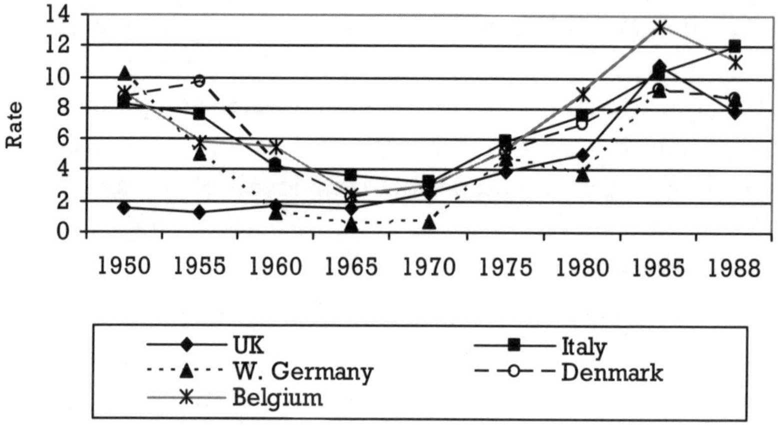

	UK	Italy
	W. Germany	Denmark
	Belgium	

Source: Mitchell, 1992; BLS.

The United States and The Netherlands (and Ireland to a certain extent) have achieved recent successes through high levels of consumer debt and spending (partly as a wealth effect for the irrational exuberance of the stock markets), such that by some measures Americans have had a negative savings rate since 1998. Certainly this is not a sustainable policy for promoting permanent full employment. In the US, it is only in the last two years of a seven-year boom that real wages have started to increase. Increases in standards of living have come through increased indebtedness. Ireland's boom has also had some of these factors (increased consumer spending and fall in savings rates). Full employment for Europe and the OECD is still a long way away and most likely unachievable in the current context.

Ireland and the New Economy

Ireland's unemployment rate followed a trend similar to Europe as a whole, yet its minimum levels in the 1960s was substantially higher than that of most European countries.

Figure 2.2: Unemployment in Ireland, 1940–88

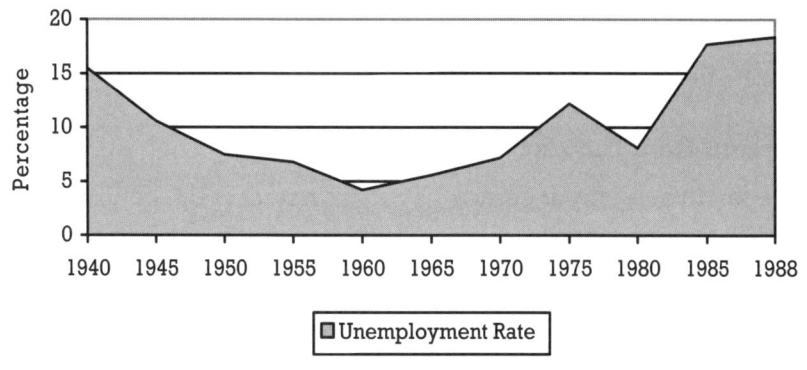

Source: Mitchell, 1992

The experience of the past decade, while encouraging for Ireland, has been rather depressing for Europe as a whole. Figure 2.3 shows the unemployment rates for Ireland and for the European Union and the OECD.

Figure 2.3: Unemployment in Ireland, the EU and OECD, 1983–2000

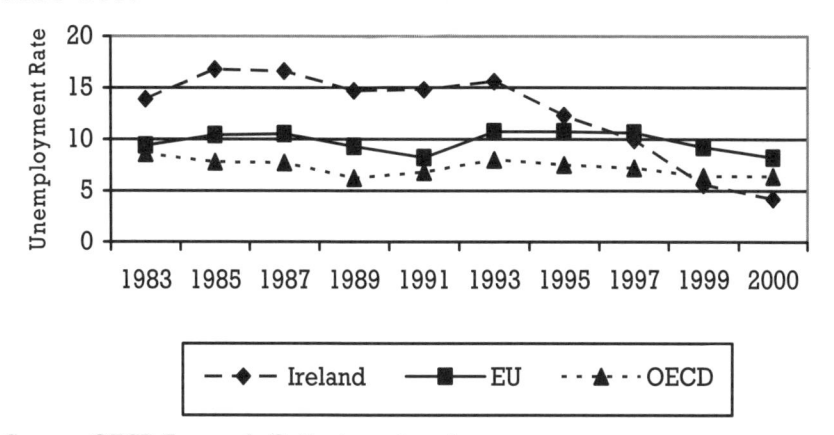

Source: *OECD Economic Outlook*, various issues.

While Ireland's unemployment rate has fallen significantly since 1992, the European Union and the OECD unemployment rates have been particularly stubborn. Given that much of Ireland's success is due to its large foreign trade surplus, it is safe to assume that Ireland will need to maintain its position as a low-cost producer — that is, to keep its labour costs below other European and OECD countries — if it wants to continue to have high employment levels. The effect of this policy is what we now turn to — stagnant wages.

Stagnant Real Incomes

It is easy to see why incomes have stagnated in the countries that still have near double-digit unemployment levels, but what is harder to understand is why incomes and wages have stagnated in the booming economies. In the US, as mentioned above, it is only after five years of economic expansion that real wages started to increase. In Ireland, much of the job growth can be attributed to the wage restraint in the last three national wage agreements (in fact, many of these agreements substituted tax cuts for wage increases). Productivity increases are not being passed on to workers in the form of higher wages, an essential component in the Keynes-Beveridge model of insuring that all benefit from economic progress. This is very clearly seen in Figure 2.4, which shows that productivity has increased 82 per cent in Ireland since 1980, while real wages have risen 20.9 per cent.

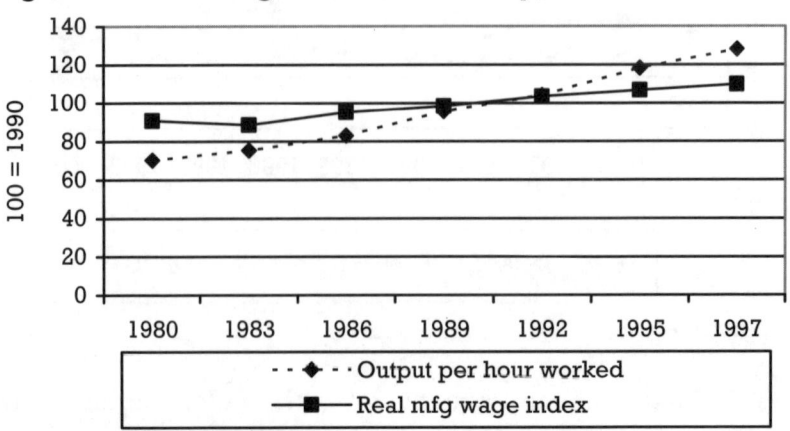

Figure 2.4: Real Wages and Productivity, 1980–97

Source: ILO Key Labour Indicators

We will return to some of these issues in Chapters 4 and 5, where competitiveness and the labour market are considered respectively. Our point here is that wage growth has not kept pace with economic progress, which is necessary if the benefits of economic progress are to be shared widely under the Keynes-Beveridge model. This failure of real wages to grow has caused households to increase their labour market activity in order to keep their standard of living from falling behind. This is an important economic factor behind the rise in the labour market participation rates of married women.

Figure 2.5: Employment to Population Ratio in Ireland, Male and Female, 1985–97

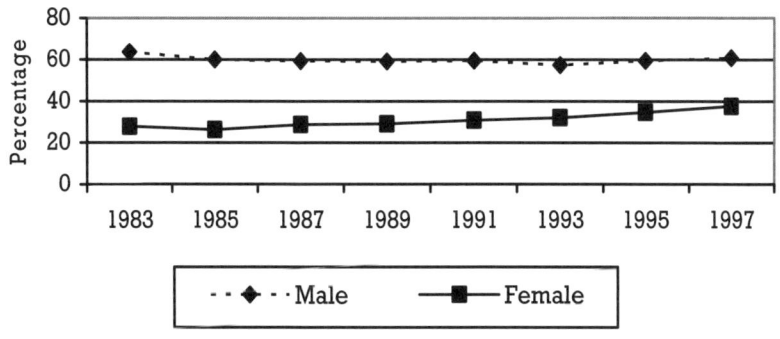

Source: ILO

The European experience suggests that a country can have rising levels of employment as long as they are willing to keep wage levels for workers stagnant (or at least well below productivity gains) as well as tolerate rising levels of income inequality and poverty (see Chapter 6), or it can pursue a policy of maintaining low levels of poverty and income inequality but sacrifice job growth.

The Death of Economic Policy

The traditional economic policy tools that were so successful in the 1950s and 1960s (but much less so in the 1970s and 1980s) became irrelevant in the 1990s. Globalisation of financial markets and the need to have "market credible" fiscal policies (as well as the constraints on these policies placed by the European Union) have greatly limited the abilities of governments to use tax and spending measures to counter the business cycle and to generate long-term economic growth. Furthermore, the end of the Bretton Woods system of fixed exchange rates has turned the world currency markets into a non-stop casino, where speculation dominates over economic fundamentals and where financial interests can discipline governments if they pursue policies that "capital" feels are imprudent (that is, hostile to their interests). This increased mobility of capital has also made it more difficult for governments to tax capital, thus shifting the burden from business and the affluent onto workers. Thus the OECD in the 1990s faced numbers of unemployed that were higher than those faced during the Great Depression, yet governments could not use Keynesian policies to fight unemployment. This situation was made worse for the European Union due to the Maastricht Treaty, which placed even greater limits on independent fiscal and monetary policy.

Furthermore, the mobility of capital, along with various trade agreements, from the GATT and WTO to the European Union, has greatly limited the ability of governments to enact or enforce microeconomic policies to generate higher real wages or better worker conditions. The European Union is, in many ways, swimming against the stream on some of these issues, for it insists that new member countries raise their standards to EU levels, rather than have a race to the bottom. This will become increasingly difficult, if not downright illegal, if the WTO is allowed to reach its proposed position as international arbitrator of the world economy. Under this new world order, some other means must be found if all are to share in the benefits being created by the new economy.

CREATING NEW INSTITUTIONS FOR THE NEW ECONOMY

The flexibility and mobility that are the chief characteristics of the new economy run counter to the structure of the welfare state, especially as it is constructed in Europe. The goals of the welfare state model are worthy goals and still need to be pursued. If the advanced capitalist economies are to remain functioning democracies and are to pursue long-term prosperity and maintain their strong civil societies, then their main challenge will be to ensure that all share in the benefits of the new economy. To understand how this can be achieved, we must first look at what is the driving force of the new economy. In this study, we will follow the lead of the NESC report mentioned in the introduction. In *Opportunities, Challenges and Capacities for Choices* (1999), four factors are highlighted as the key characteristics of "globalisation": technology, trade liberalisation, increased capital mobility (capital/financial flows) and labour market flexibility. In the remainder of this chapter we will discuss each of these factors, specifically in terms of their role in Basic Income policies.

Technology

Not a day seems to go by without a new technological marvel being heralded in the press. No doubt the pace of technological change has been accelerating, much like it did for the first "great transformation". At such a quick pace, it is no wonder that most analysts have not looked at the potential long-term economic implications of these advances. As the technology goes through a radical transformation, we should expect that other economic and social institutions will also have to be transformed.

Looking back at the first Great Transformation and the changes that it prompted in society and the economy, and the response of economists, gives us a good perspective on our current situation (though there are admittedly major significant differences). The technological changes at the beginning of the 19th century were very disruptive to English society. While the new factory systems were generating dramatic productivity increases, they also created considerable strain on the fabric of society. One of these major strains was the elimination of many skilled job categories. Many of these job categories were held by adult men and paid a family wage. Yet the new technology did not require their now outdated skills, and the factory owners preferred women and children for factory employment over adult men. The use of machines and mechanical power greatly reduced the need for physically strong men and skilled workers. Women and children could be controlled more easily and could be paid much less. This forced whole families to enter the labour force, as the income from all was needed to support the family unit. The most dramatic reaction to this trend was the "Luddites", a movement of workers who would break into factories in the night and smash up the machines that they felt had replaced them. The abuses and cruelty of this new economy became a major theme in the literature of the 19th century as well as an essential component in the critique of capitalism by Karl Marx and other critics.[1] So paramount had this problem become that even David Ricardo, whose economics is almost completely immune from any empirical grounding and who was no friend or advocate of the poor and workers, was forced to admit the negative side of the new technology, adding the famous Chapter 31 "On Machinery" to the third edition of his *Principles of Political Economy and Taxation* in 1821. The new economy of the early 19th century produced considerable benefits and costs; the benefits went to the owners of businesses and the landed rich while the costs were born by workers, women and children and the poor. The next 150 years of social legislation, from the Factory Acts to limit the exploitation of women and children to the legalisation of unions and the creation of the welfare state, was an attempt, mostly successful but long in coming, to ensure that all benefited from the new economy. However, as noted earlier in this chapter, the rules are changing once again, and technology is a prime mover in these changes.

The problem of "technological unemployment" in the first great transformation was settled in two ways. One, those who believed in *laissez-faire* economics felt that the new technology would create more jobs than it destroyed. The positive net job creation in the face of rapid technological advances was achieved through a rapid growth in the population of England and Wales from 8.9 million in 1801 to 17.9 million in 1851; a demographic shift from rural to urban (who are less self-sufficient and thus require more produced goods and services); and a low standard of living starting point. There was therefore a large amount of unmet material needs. Thus, in the aggregate, the number of new jobs exceeded those displaced, although the new jobs frequently didn't go to those who had been displaced. This led to the second phase in dealing with "technological unemployment": the market was given free reign to eliminate surplus and shortages of factors of production, including workers. New workers frequently got the new jobs, older workers were cast aside, their higher morality rates and short longevity erasing the disequilibrium in the labour market.

All will agree that this method of eliminating labour surpluses would not be acceptable today. Yet the changes in the technology of production have the potential to generate technological unemployment at an unprecedented scale. The current boom in the Irish economy and the record job growth should not blind us to these long-run trends. Neither Ireland, nor her trading partners, will experience the rate of population growth or the demographic shift that allowed the industrial revolution to proceed. Furthermore, Ireland and her trading partners are already "affluent societies", a long way removed from the supply-constrained economies of the 18th and early 19th centuries. The unlimited demand of the 19th century is gone, replaced by the artificially generated and manipulated demand of advertisers and consumerism. The environmental realities of the 21st century greatly increase the costs and dangers of using conspicuous consumption and conspicuous waste to keep the economic engine of capitalism running at full speed.

While there is still unmet material need in the poor communities of the rich countries and, of course, in the vast majority of the world's population living in squalor in the third world, there is little hope of a trickling down of the benefits of the new economy to these masses. As we see in Chapter 6 of this book, the poor are being left out of the new economy; this is even more true in the other countries that have fully embraced the logic of globalism: the United States, Canada and the United Kingdom. Thus we will not have an "unlimited demand" option.

Given the already existing excess capacity in the world manufacturing economy, and the dramatic labour-saving technological developments of the past decade (see Jeremy Rifkin's *The End of Work* for a sober assessment of these developments), Ireland's continued economic successes can only come by out-competing her trading partners. There will be no rising tide lifting all boats. Technological change is never socially neutral; the key is how the benefits of these technological developments will be shared by all. They can allow for a reduction in the amount of time a household has to work to support a decent standard of living, increasing time for leisure and community and social activities, or they can lead to a greater pressure to work more hours, running faster merely to maintain one's standard of living. The key is whether social and economic institutions adjust to the new realities, with one of the most important being the institutions that distribute the benefits of economic progress. This is exactly what a Basic Income proposes to do. It takes a small share of overall output and distributes it to all, ensuring that all share in the benefits of economic activity. It also supports the lower end of the labour market, as discussed in Chapter 6. The old rules lead to a winner-take-all situation, or require micro-management to achieve equitable results (thus running the risk of stifling economic progress).

Trade Liberalisation

Trade liberalisation is a fact of the new economy. The only question is whether it will be limited to regional trade agreements or to a global system (as proposed with the WTO). Our concern is why trade liberalisation is important for a Basic Income system. One of the ways that countries have ensured that the benefits of economic progress filter down to workers and the poor in their countries has been by protecting these workers from competition. Unions do this nationally, but in an international economy this is achieved through trade policy. There are two basic forms of trade policy: tariffs and trade barriers, and currency policy. Tariffs and trade barriers provide protection for workers and businesses in that they reduce the potential for low-cost producers supplying goods to their customers. Currency policy allows the government or central bank to reduce the cost of production domestically by lowering the exchange rate of the currency (this also makes foreign goods more expensive).

The euro eliminates the possibility of Ireland unilaterally attempting to manipulate its currency to achieve a better balance of trade (although the euro region as a whole can attempt this), and increased capital mobility had already seriously reduced this option. As for the former form of trade policy, the move towards more international trade agreements limits the use of this tool. Thus, two of the important tools to raise the standards of living of workers and to ensure that all benefit in economic progress have been partially or completely eliminated. A new set of institutions is needed to ensure that the benefits of the new economy will be widely shared.

Capital Mobility

Few can doubt the benefits to Ireland of capital mobility in the 1990s. Foreign direct investment (FDI) has been the prime driver of the "Celtic Tiger" economy. Yet one has to be aware of the various downsides to capital mobility. Before capital became so mobile, the fact that factories could not be so easily moved overseas, and that managing overseas operations was problematic, allowed workers to benefit from growth in output. This point was noted by Adam Smith in *The Wealth of Nations*, where he notes that business will tend to invest in home markets over foreign investment (which he felt was more risky). As Ireland never had much capital to invest, the old rules did not benefit Ireland all that much. It neither had large amounts of money, nor a large and strong domestic market to justify much investment. For the various reasons discussed in Chapter 4, Ireland now benefits from foreign investment. Yet, as we have seen in the numerous financial crises of the 1990s, large inflows in FDI can easily turn into large outflows, at speeds Adam Smith could not have imagined. The increased capital mobility has led to a weakening in the relative power of workers, as discussed in Chapters 5 and 6. One of the manifestations of this is the fall in the share of income going to labour and the rise in the share going to capital. Another manifestation of the change in the rules of the economy due to the increased mobility of capital is the rise in real interest rates due to the higher level of risk and uncertainty in the post-Bretton Woods world. This too contributes to more income inequality. More than any other development of the new economy, the increased capital mobility has weakened the relative position of workers, thus promoting greater income inequality. Short of massive international capital controls, some other means needs to be devised for more equitably distributing the benefits of economic progress.

Labour Market Flexibility

As with the other factors mentioned above, a key method of spreading the benefits of economic progress down the economic ladder has been through the regulation of labour markets, either by the government or by unions. Many of these regulations are only successful to the extent that they create rigidities. These rigidities allow wages to rise with the cost being shifted to another sector (either a fall in profits or higher prices).[2] These regulations benefit the workers in question, but often shift the cost onto consumers (another set of workers). This process runs the risk of getting out of control and leading to generalised inflation (as was experienced in the 1970s). In

Chapter 5, we examine in more depth the issue of labour market flexibility. The point we want to make here is that labour market flexibility reduces the ability to distribute the benefits of economic progress widely, thus furthering the case for the need for new institutions to achieve this, such as a Basic Income system.

Conclusion

Ireland has a unique opportunity. The new economy will force change in social and economic institutions. That cannot be denied. What that change will be, however, is an open question. If we follow the example of history, the new institutions will be created by and for those with the most power and control in the "new economy", shifting the costs, both economic and social, onto the weak and powerless, the poor, workers, families and communities. These interests will push for greater labour market flexibilities without security; increased stress on families without support; and weakening of the social bonds that hold communities together. Such developments will be shortsighted, for although they will increase the wealth of the rich and powerful in the short run, they will undermine the essential social and family relationships that form the foundation of prosperous societies. They will foster social decay, family breakup, increased crime, rising poverty and social exclusion[3] — the "Americanisation" of society to go along with the "Brazilianisation" of the economy. We should have no doubts that these changes will prompt a "backlash", just as the changes created by the Industrial Revolution prompted decades of social struggle by those who had the costs of their new economy hoisted onto their shoulders and had their social institutions stressed and threatened, a backlash that ended with the creation of the welfare state. Ireland can choose to skip the pain and suffering and simultaneously adjust its social and economic institutions along with the changes brought about by globalisation and technological change, to share both the costs and benefits of the new economy. It is just this goal that Basic Income systems are designed to do.

In many ways, something like a Basic Income system is inevitable if Europe seeks to achieve the dynamic economy that technological change and globalisation offer while maintaining the commitment to social justice and a civil and humane society. Each European Union country has a complex social welfare system that is testament to each respective country's commitment to these laudable goals. However, as European economic integration progresses, especially with the introduction of the euro, it will become increasingly problematic to sustain a unified economy with each country having vastly different social welfare systems. Further economic and political integration will require a harmonisation of social welfare systems. A Basic Income system set up at European level will achieve just this. Towards this end, Ireland can take the lead in showing how best to achieve a dynamic economy that maintains its commitment to social justice and a civil and humane society.

Endnotes

[1] Chapters 10 and 15 of *Das Kapital* (Marx, 1867) are essential reading for anyone who wants to understand this topic.

[2] If wages only go up as much as worker productivity then there is no pressure to raise prices or shift costs; yet there is no automatic mechanism to achieve this, thus productivity increases will only be passed on to workers if they have the market power to capture them.

[3] Ironically, these changes will increase the statistical measures of economic progress, such as GDP, as they reduce the quality of life, thus giving the impression that things are improving while they continue to get worse (see Clark and Kavanagh (1996), "Progress, Values and Economic Indicators" in *Progress, Values and Public Policy,* edited by Brigid Reynolds and Sean Healy, (Dublin: CORI), pp. 60–92.

Chapter 3

A BASIC INCOME GUARANTEE PROPOSAL

INTRODUCTION

In order to fully discuss how a Basic Income system would allow Ireland to adjust to the realities of the "new economy", we need to actually develop a Basic Income proposal. The Basic Income proposal presented here has three core elements: Basic Income Payments, the Social Solidarity Fund and a new tax system. There are many variations of how a Basic Income system might be introduced in Ireland, with endless variation in each of these three core elements. In this chapter, we develop an example of a Basic Income system that meets the goals and values outlined in Chapter 1. Any actual Basic Income system that would be introduced in Ireland will necessarily be the result of extensive discussion and negotiation between the government, the social partners and eventually by the citizenry. The purpose of developing a detailed example of how a Basic Income system in Ireland might work is to allow a detailed discussion of the specifics of what such a system would mean in the context of the Irish economy and Irish society. Only with a detailed proposal, even a hypothetical one, can we then discuss the issues of the equity and efficiency effects of a Basic Income policy in Ireland. These issues are discussed in Chapters 4, 5 and 6. In Chapter 7, we will look at some of the trade-offs that arise with variations in the basic elements — specifically, benefit levels and funding the system.

AN EXAMPLE OF AN IRISH BASIC INCOME SYSTEM

As stated above, any Basic Income system has three core elements: a Basic Income payment; a system of social support for those the Basic Income system does not lift out of poverty (in this proposal, the Social Solidarity Fund); and a system for funding the Basic Income system. If the Basic Income payment levels are designed as a full Basic Income system, where the benefit levels are at the official poverty rates, then the need for something like a Social Solidarity Fund diminishes.

Our Basic Income proposal is based on the fiscal year 2001/2002. All of our cost estimates come from official government sources (mostly taken from Budget 2001 and the Revenue Commissioners) or else we have used the estimates provided by the ESRI, taken from either their *Medium-Term Review, 1999–2005* (1999) or from their contributions to the Working Group on Basic Income Study.

Payment Levels

Our Basic Income Proposal would have the following Basic Income Payments for the fiscal year 2001/2002. These payments would be universal and not subject to taxation.

Table 3.1: Basic Income Payments 2001 (per week in €)

Age	Payment
80+	142.21
65 to 79	135.86
18 to 64	109.20
0 to 17	43.17

Our population estimates are based on the CSO October 1999 estimates, and are based on an additional 2 per cent growth in population for the year 2001 (keeping the demographic breakdown constant). With the population estimates, we can calculate

A Basic Income Guarantee Proposal

the full cost of the Basic Income payments. These are provided in Table 3.2 below.

Table 3.2: Cost of Basic Income Payments, 2001 (in €)

Age	Per Week (€)	Annual (€)	Population (thousands)	Costs (€ millions)
80 plus	142.21	7,414.86	81.9	607.27
65 to 79	135.86	7,083.84	350.6	2,483.59
18 to 64	109.20	5,693.56	2,343.0	13,340.01
0 to 17	43.17	2,250.94	1,002.2	2,255.89
Total			3,777.7	18,686.76

The total cost of Basic Income payments in 2001/02 would be €18,686.76 million.

Cost of Social Solidarity Fund

As our Basic Income payment levels are not all at the official poverty levels, some low-income households will have their income fall slightly. To counter this, we propose introducing a Social Solidarity Fund, designed to compensate any low-income households that might be adversely affected by the implementation of the Basic Income system. As one of the primary goals of a Basic Income system is to help those in low income, it is an explicit goal not to lower the disposable income of any low-income households. The implementation of the Social Solidarity Fund is beyond the scope of this book. It would cost about €104 million to compensate all households below the 50 per cent poverty threshold for any losses due to the implementation of the Basic Income Proposal, well under the amount budgeted by our proposal. The net cost of the Social Solidarity Fund in 2001 is estimated at €804.90 million. This is itemised in the following table.

Table 3.3: Cost of Social Solidarity Fund, 2001

Items	Cost € million
Supplementary Welfare System	308.66
Additional anti-poverty payments	95.84
Additional payments to the elderly	273.43
Optical, dental, aural	45.10
Assistance with mortgages	35.24
Socially useful work	126.97
Savings on interim payments	(80.34)
Total	804.90

Cost of Other Government Services

Our Basic Income proposal eliminates the need for much of the current Government spending on social welfare and also eliminates the income tax and PSRI tax systems. To calculate how much revenue our new tax system must generate, we must first calculate how much additional government spending there will be (besides the spending on the Basic Income system).

Table 3.4: Costs of Funding Other Government Services, 2001 (Post-2001 Budget Numbers)

Estimated Revenue on:	(€ million)
Income Tax	9,878.56
PRSI Receipts	3,315.29
Total Revenue to be replaced	13,193.85
Net Exchequer Expenditure on Welfare	(7,813.97)
Other Government Services*	5,379.88

* The Balance required to fund other government services (€13,193.85m − €7,813.97m) = €5,379.88m.

A Basic Income Guarantee Proposal

In the Basic Income proposal being presented here, we have not made any other adjustments to government spending and the projected surpluses.

Table 3.5: Savings Incurred by the Basic Income Plan (1999; 2001)

	1999 Costs (€m)	1999 Saved by BI (€m)	2001 Cost (€m)	2001 Saved by BI (€m)
Community Employment Programme	417.74	417.74	463.70	463.70
Third level and ESF trainees	123.16	123.16	136.71	136.71
Agricultural income supports	285.69	285.69	316.80	316.80
Employment and training grants (FAS)	69.84	69.84	77.52	77.52
Administrative savings in Department of SW	255.22	128.24	283.29	142.35
Total	1,151.65	1,024.67	1,278.02	1,137.08

Net Costs of Basic Income Proposal

The net cost is calculated by adding the costs of the Basic Income payments, with the costs of the social solidarity fund and the balance required to fund other government services, plus the addition of the Administrative Costs, and then subtract the savings incurred by the Basic Income system.

Table 3.6: Net Costs of Basic Income System, 2001 (€m)

Basic Income Costs	18,686.77
Social Solidarity Fund	804.90
Other Govt.	5,379.88
Savings	(1,137.08)
Administration	141.08
Net Costs	23,875.55

FINANCING THE BASIC INCOME PLAN

In estimating the tax rate to finance the proposed Basic Income system, we first have to estimate the tax base for 2001/02. The Revenue Commissioners have provided the tax base estimates for the years 1998/99 through 2001/02, based on their projections as of the summer of 1998. Therefore, the estimates provided here should be considered on the conservative side, as the actual tax base has been generally exceeding projections.

Estimating the Tax Base

The following are the tax base figures as provided by the Revenue Commissioners.

Table 3.7: Unadjusted Tax Base, 1998/99 – 2001/2002*

Year	Tax Base (unadjusted)
1998/1999	€34,178.81 million
1999/2000	€37,762.01 million
2000/2001	€41,545.83 million
2001/2002	€45,243.31 million

* Memo, 20 June 2000, Revenue Commissioners

Under a Basic Income system, some items that are currently included in the tax base will need to be excluded, and some items which are currently excluded will need to be included; thus, the estimates of the tax base provided by the Revenue Commissioners need to be adjusted. These additions and subtractions were suggested in a Memo, dated 30 September 1998, from the Revenue Commissioners. As some of the items listed include estimates from 1995, 1996 and 1997, these estimates need to be adjusted for the final year of implementation (2001/2002). The following table provides the list provided by the Revenue Commissioners, with their original estimates, plus adjustments for 2001/2002 using two adjustment factors: the consumer price index (CPI) and growth in the tax base. The most accurate method of adjusting these items is to make adjustments based on each specific item's growth relative to growth in the tax base. This method, however, would be very time-consuming and costly, and might not be possible anyway. This book adopts the estimates based on growth in the tax base, as this is most closely linked with the factors under consideration. We have also added back into the tax base the €126.97 million to be spent on socially useful work in the social solidarity fund, as this income would be subject to taxation under the proposed Basic Income system.

Table 3.8: Revenue Commissioner's Adjustments to Revenue Tax Base for Basic Income, 2001/02

Adjustment Items (Base year)	Original Estimates (€m)	Adjustments by CPI 2001/02 (€m)	Adjustments by Growth in Tax Base 2001/02 (€m)
Subtractions:			
Capital Allowances (1995/96)	−474.88	−522.37	−669.53
Losses (1995/96)	−91.42	−100.56	−128.88
Social Welfare Pension Income est. (2001/02)	−714.86	−714.86	−714.86
Total Subtractions	**−1,281.17**	**−1,337.80**	**−1,513.27**
Additions:			
Employees' Contributions to Pension Funds (1995)	399.97	447.96	564.40
Interest on Savings Cert. etc. (1995/96)	78.72	86.60	110.98
Deposit Interest income undeclared or not recorded (1995/96)	492.66	541.92	694.67
Exempt income in statutory redundancy payments (1997/98)	34.28	36.31	48.38
Income exempt under share schemes (1995/96)	40.63	44.69	57.27
Exempt income of artists & writers (1995/96)	27.93	30.73	39.36
Rented Residential Relief (1996/97)	44.44	48.00	62.73
Income of Farmers and other self-employed not on record est. (2001/02)	352.99	352.99	352.99
Total Additions	**1,471.63**	**1,589.20**	**1,930.78**
Less Total Subtractions	−1,281.17	−1,337.80	−1,513.27
Plus Income from Socially Useful Work (2001/02)	126.97	126.97	126.97
Net Adjustments to Revenue Base	**317.43**	**378.38**	**544.48**

Table 3.9: Adjusted Revenue Commissioner's Projected Tax Base, 2001

Year	Tax Base (€m)
2001/02	45,243.31 + 544.48 = 45,787.79

Social Responsibility Tax

The Social Responsibility Tax is implemented to replace the current system of employer PSRI taxation, which in our proposal is eliminated along with the income tax system. It is estimated based on projected growth in the Tax Base as forecasted by the Revenue Commissioners. It is based on an 8.5 per cent rate, equal to the current Employer PSRI levels.

Table 3.10: Social Responsibility Tax, 2001

Year	Social Responsibility Tax (€m)
2001	2,289.34

Calculating the Tax Rate for the Basic Income System in 2001/02

Calculating the necessary tax rate for financing the Basic Income System under consideration here is straightforward. You take the net cost of the system (which includes the funding of other government services) and subtract the revenue from the social responsibility tax. You then calculate what the necessary tax rate that generates sufficient income to pay for the Basic Income system.

In 2001, the net costs are projected to be:	€23,875.55m
Subtract the Social Responsibility Tax	– €2,289.34m
Amount necessary to finance out of flat tax	€21,586.21m

With a tax base of €45,787.79 million in 2001, a flat tax of **47.14 per cent** is what is required to fund the Basic Income system proposed here.

Chapter 4

BASIC INCOME AND COMPETITIVENESS

INTRODUCTION

In the next two chapters we will look at how our proposed Basic Income system would impact on the competitiveness of the Irish economy. In considering the subject of how a change in social policy will impact the competitiveness of an economy, we must keep in mind that we can only look at these issues indirectly. There is not an exact science as to what promotes or retards the competitiveness of an economy or, for that matter, how social policies influence the competitiveness of an economy. This does not mean that policy analysts cannot offer a rational analysis of the economic implications of social policy. What it does mean is that the best one can hope for is to examine all the issues that are accepted as central to the competitiveness of the Irish economy and attempt to ascertain how these factors will be affected by the implementation of a Basic Income policy such as the one developed in Chapter 3. It also means that, when examining an issue like Basic Income, or any economic policy for that matter, the analysts must be open and honest about the assumptions they make, the issues they feel are important for consideration, the data and models used to investigate possible economic outcomes and the relevance of the issues being discussed.

In this chapter, we will concentrate on how a Basic Income policy would influence the competitiveness of the Irish economy. We will do this by first reviewing the factors that are credited with promoting Ireland's recent economic successes, concentrating on a traditional macroeconomic view of competitiveness. However, to get a deeper understanding of what influences competitiveness — that is, what is behind (or the causes of) the macroeconomic results — we must take a more microeconomic view. Here we will follow the path taken by the National Competitiveness Council, and investigate how a Basic Income policy would affect the numerous individual economic and social factors which, taken together, the National Competitiveness Council feels determine the competitiveness of the Irish economy. In the next chapter, we will concentrate on how our proposed Basic Income system would affect the Irish labour market. As the labour market impacts are an important aspect of the issue of competitiveness, there will be a certain amount of overlap between Chapters 4 and 5. In this chapter, we will mostly look at labour as a cost factor in business competitiveness, leaving the issues of unemployment, wage inequality, labour supply and demand and participation rates to the next chapter.

IRELAND'S RECENT ECONOMIC SUCCESSES

Before looking at the factors that have contributed to Ireland's recent economic successes, it is worth briefly reviewing the rather remarkable recent developments in the Irish economy. Over the past seven years, Ireland has had the fastest growing economy, as measured by changes in GDP, in Europe and among the developed countries of the OECD. Figure 4.1 shows the growth in real GDP for Ireland, for the OECD as a whole and for the Euro Area.

Keeping in mind all of the usual caveats that are mentioned when discussing Ireland's GDP estimates, Ireland has been outperforming the rest of the developed world at least since 1993. During this period, Ireland's unemployment rate has fallen from over 15 per cent to under 4 per cent in 2001. The fall in Irish unemployment is more remarkable when one considers that the unemployment rate for the Euro Area countries remained above 10 per cent through 1999 and only recently fell below double digits. (We saw some of the trends in unemployment in Chapter 2 and we will return to this topic in Chapter 5.) This economic growth has played an important role in the reduction of the net indebtedness of the Government, from a peak of 112.1 per cent of GDP in 1987 to an estimate of 32.7 per cent for 2001. It is no wonder economists have become fascinated with the "Celtic Tiger".

Figure 4.1: Growth Rates for Ireland, OECD and Euro Area, 1973–2001

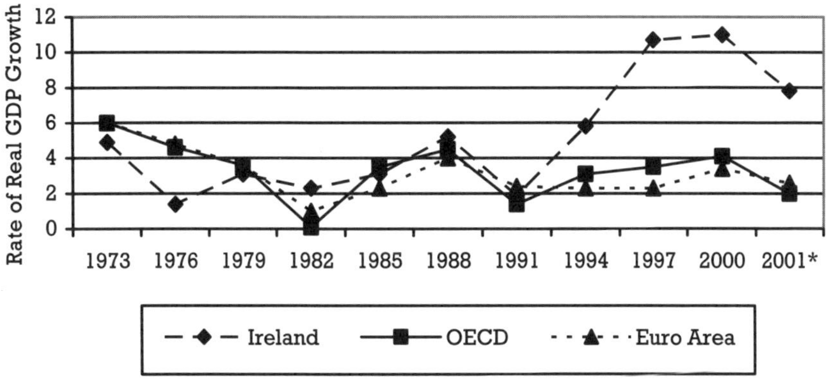

* Projection

Source: OECD Economic Outlook, various issues.

FACTORS THAT CONTRIBUTED TO THE CELTIC TIGER

The most outstanding characteristic of the so-called "Celtic Tiger" economy has been the fall in the rate of unemployment, from over 15 per cent in 1992 to 3.8 per cent in September 2000. What makes this even more remarkable is that this is at a time of little employment growth in Europe (see Figure 4.2). Growth in employment is fairly easy to explain. More people have jobs when there is an increase in the demand for the goods and services that these people, if employed, would produce. Our interest in this chapter is to investigate how a Basic Income policy would impact on the factors that have produced these results. Thus, we will first look at the rise in aggregate demand that produced the fall in unemployment and then, secondly, what impact a Basic Income policy would have on the microeconomic factors that promoted these outstanding macroeconomic results.

MACROECONOMICS OF THE "CELTIC TIGER"

Variations in Ireland's rates of unemployment can easily be explained by looking at changes in the level of aggregate demand (see Clark, 1998, for a theoretical explanation). In Table 4.1 below, we see the average rate of change for various components of aggregate demand and the unemployment rates for three time periods: 1973–79, 1980–93 and 1994–99. The final column takes the average figures for the period 1996–99.

Table 4.1: Rates of Change in Irish Aggregate Demand, 1973–99

Average Annual Growth in:	1973–79	1980–93	1994–99	1996–99
Real Private Consumption	4.2	2.0	6.2	7.3
Real Public Consumption	5.5	1.0	4.0	4.3
Total Gross Fixed Investment	6.8	–0.4	14.6	11.3
Total Domestic Demand	3.4	1.3	7.8	8.6
Real Exports	8.5	8.6	15.9	15.3
Real Imports	9.2	4.6	15.7	15.8
Unemployment Rate*	7.3	14.1	10.4	7.1

*Unemployment Rate is the average for each time period.

Source: OECD Economic Outlook, various years.

From Table 4.1, we see the factors that led to the dramatic rise in unemployment during the 1980s, the fall in private consumption from a 4.2 per cent rate of growth in the 1973–79 period to 2.0 per cent in the 1980–93 period, and the even more dramatic fall in public consumption (from 5.5 per cent growth rate to 1.0 per cent) and the most dramatic change of all, the reduction of the total gross fixed investment growth rate, from a healthy 6.8 per cent (which helped to bring Irish unemployment levels in the late 1970s down to European levels) to a –0.4 per cent rate of change during the 1980s and early 1990s. Any country that is disinvesting will certainly have a rise in unemployment. These all changed around in the 1994–99 period, where private consumption rose to a 6.2 per cent rate of growth, public consumption increased to 4.0 per cent and, most importantly, total gross fixed investment went from negative changes to an average rate of increase of 14.6 per cent, leading to a rise in the rate of growth in total domestic demand from a rate of 1.3 per cent during the 1980–93 period to 7.8 per cent in 1994–99. One does not have to be John Maynard Keynes to figure out that these changes will lead to rapid job growth.

This close association between aggregate demand and unemployment rates is again seen in Figure 4.2 below, which looks at the relationship between real total domestic demand and the unemployment rate. It is clear from this graph that when the growth in domestic demand falls below a certain level, the rate of unemployment increases, and when it rises above a certain level, unemployment falls. (This critical level is not a fixed value, as the economy is not a machine that merely responds to stimuli in fixed proportions, but is an evolving set of processes where context determines how the economy adjusts to changes.) When Ireland's growth in domestic demand was higher than that of the Euro Area average, its unemployment performance exceeded that of the Euro Area, with the reverse relationship being true as well.

Figure 4.2: Domestic Demand and Unemployment Rates, Ireland and Euro Area, 1973–2000

- Ireland Unemployment Rate
- Euro Area Unemployment Rate
- Ireland Domestic Demand
- Euro Area Domestic Demand

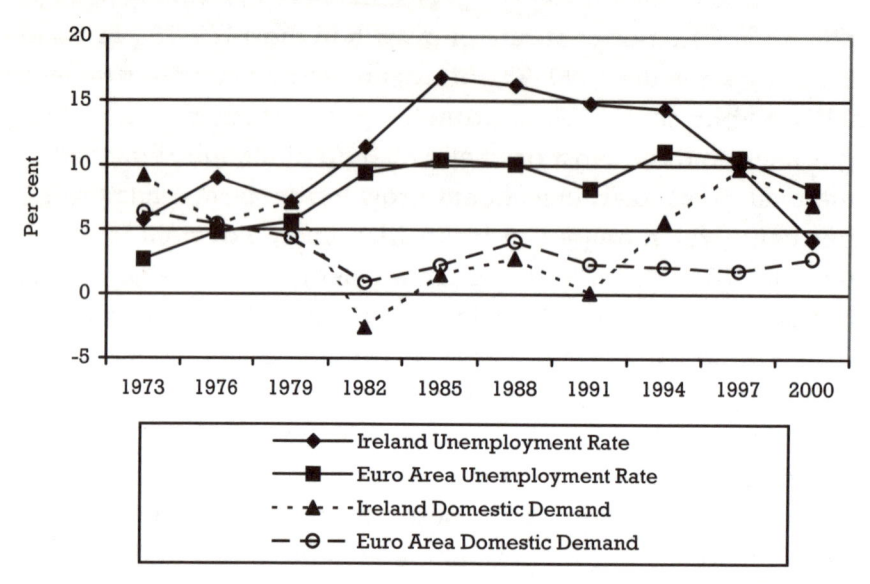

Growth in Investment

As stated above, the increase in total gross fixed investment has been the most dramatic factor in promoting economic growth in Ireland. This is seen below in Figure 4.3.

Figure 4.3: Changes in Total Gross Fixed Capital Formation in Ireland, 1983–2001

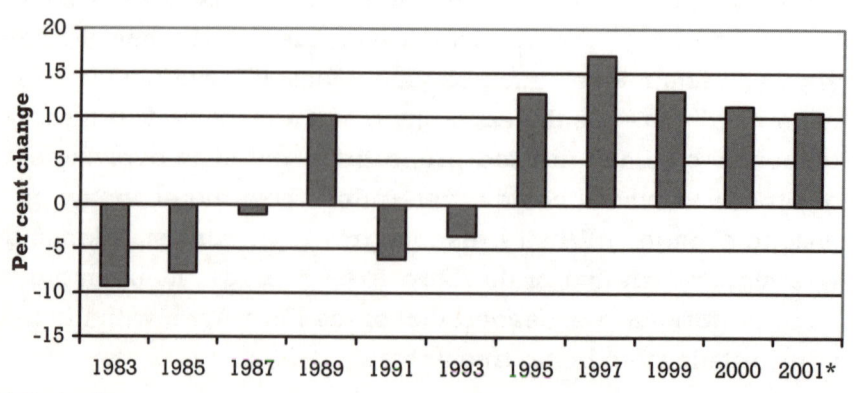

* Projection.
Source: OECD Economic Outlook, various years.

Much of the gross fixed investment has come from foreign firms investing in Ireland and to a lesser extent from the Structural Funds and Common Agricultural Policy from the European Union, which have accounted for "a staggering £12 [€15.24] billion since 1990 alone, equal to a free gift of £3,500 [€4,444.08] to every person in Ireland. Few countries have ever received *largesse* on such a grand scale" (McAleese, 1997, p. 2). In fact, it has been noted that in "1995, FDI (Foreign Direct Investment) into Ireland accounted for 20.2 per cent of GDP" (O'Connor, Walsh and Owens, 1998, p. 1) which is much higher than the EU average for the same year of 13.3 per cent. The impact of this foreign flow of investment has been widely noted: "Subsidiaries of foreign multinationals account for one out of every two jobs in Irish manufacturing, and for 40 per cent of [Ireland's] export earnings" (McAleese, 1997, p. 2).

Foreign Trade

Changes in total domestic demand only show part of the aggregate demand story, as exports and imports are also very important, especially in a small open economy like Ireland. The rate of growth in real exports is partially the result of Irish competitiveness and partly the result of the rate of economic growth in Ireland's leading trading partners. In Figure 4.4, we see changes in Ireland's balance of trade from 1983 to 1999. Here we see a large increase in the surplus during the recent period of rapid employment growth.

Figure 4.4: Trade Balance (Net Exports), Ireland, 1982-2001

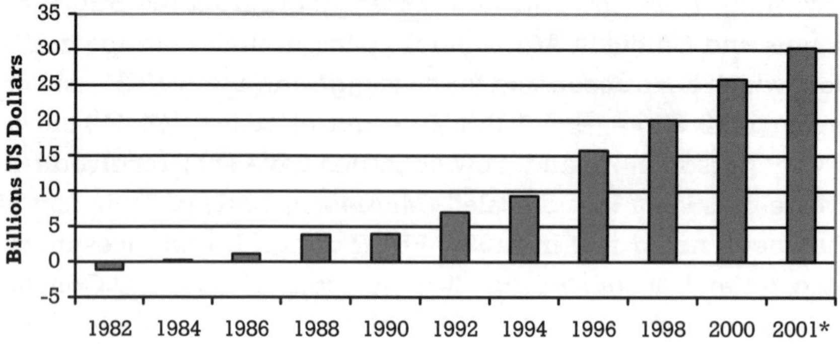

* Projected
Source: OECD Economic Outlook, 1991, 2001

Thus we can see that both domestic and foreign demand for Irish goods and services have been rising. But the benefits of the foreign sector to Ireland's recent economic growth are not limited to export growth. Looking at the data above, the logical question is: why has Ireland's trade balance improved so much in the past six years, and why have levels of Foreign Direct Investment grown so rapidly in Ireland in the past decade? Dermot McAleese (1997, p. 2) has given the following reasons:

> Foreign investors are attracted to Ireland for several reasons. First, our access to the EU and other foreign markets enables them to use Ireland as a platform from which to export to these markets. (The Irish market on its own is far too small to attract any significant volume of inward manufacturing investment.) Second, the availability of an ambitious, flexible and motivated Irish workforce also encourages inward investment. Third, overseas investors have been attracted by Ireland's low corporate taxes.

The second factor, labour, is what is important for us. In Table 4.2 we see the cost of labour in Ireland compared with other developed countries.

Basic Income and Competitiveness   59

Table 4.2: Total Hourly Compensation Costs in US$ for Production Workers in Manufacturing, 1998

Country	Total
Ireland	13.3
United Kingdom	16.4
France	18.3
Germany	27.2
Netherlands	20.6
Spain	12.1
USA	18.6
Japan	18.1

Irish competitiveness, in terms of labour costs, is seen also in Figures 4.5 and 4.6. Figure 4.5 depicts the trends in unit labour cost for Ireland and its trading partners from 1985 up to 2002, while Figure 4.6 gives a comparison between Ireland's labour costs and the labour costs of the OECD and EU.

Figure 4.5: Unit Wage Costs, Ireland and Major Trading Partners, 1985–2002 (1990 equals 100)

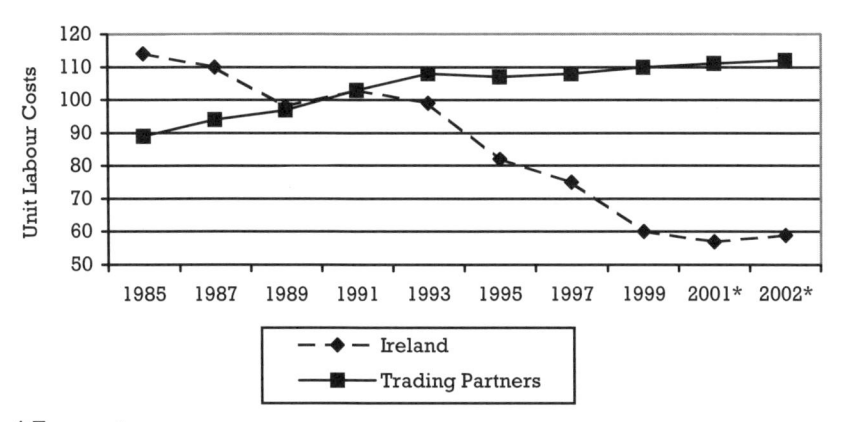

*Forecast
Source: *Central Bank of Ireland Quarterly Bulletin*, various issues

Figure 4.6: Trends in Labour Costs, Ireland, OECD and EU (US = 100)

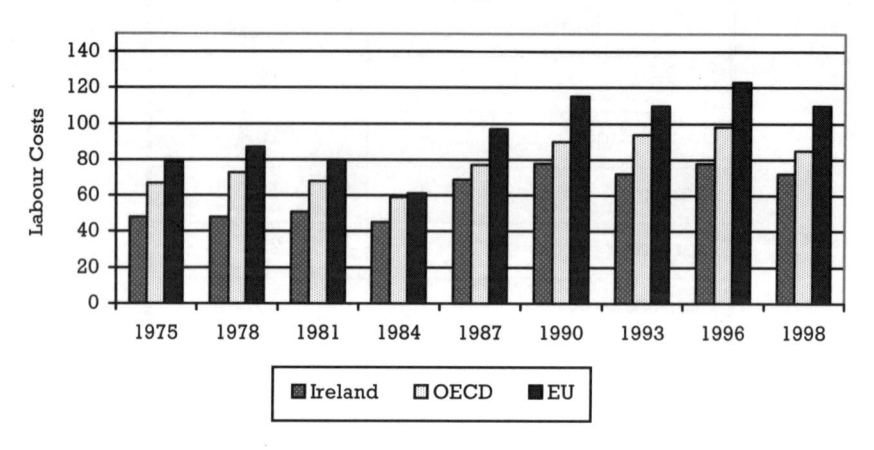

[Bar chart showing Labour Costs for Ireland, OECD, and EU from 1975 to 1998, with US = 100]

Source: US Department of Labor, 2000.

MICROECONOMIC FACTORS OF THE "CELTIC TIGER"

The Annual Competitiveness Reports published by the National Competitiveness Council have greatly raised the level of discussion and analysis on the issue of the competitiveness of the Irish economy. Their approach is to highlight factors that they assert are important for competitiveness, or that are important indicators of competitiveness (or the lack thereof) and to measure Ireland's performance in relation to the countries Ireland is competing against. It is an approach that is similar to that taken by Lester Thurow of MIT in his well-known book, *Head to Head* (1992), which compared the performance of the US economy and society with that of Europe and Japan. One can certainly disagree with the inclusion, exclusion and/or interpretation of each particular indicator, as is always the case in any ambitious project, but one cannot quibble with the importance and usefulness of their efforts in informing the public discourse on these critical issues. While noting that "competition happens at the level of the individual enterprise — or even at the level of a strategic business unit within a larger enterprise" (NCC, 2000, p. i) the Council recognises that all business takes place within a larger context, one that is a complex mixture of economic, social, political and culture factors. They have set out what they call "critical competitiveness priorities" which are arranged into seven categories: Social Partnership; People; Costs; Infrastructure; Telecommunications and E-Business; Competition and Regulation; and Science and Technology. The first three of these categories are relevant to the issue of Basic Income, thus we will limit our attention to these (with Social Partnership being considered below, and most of the People and Costs issues being considered in the next chapter, as these are labour market issues). It should be noted that the NCC purpose and ours are very different. The NCC is interested in looking at each indicator to see how Ireland has performed relative to the countries they have designated as competitors. Our interest is first to evaluate these indicators as a measure of competitiveness and second to see how a Basic Income policy would affect their outcome.

Social Partnership

The central role of social partnership in Ireland's economic strategy for reversing the economic declines of the late 1970s and 1980s was "based on the insight that moderate wage growth would underpin international competitiveness, reverse the cycle of pressures on the public finances and, by reducing inflationary pressures, lend credibility to the exchange rate strategy reflected in membership of the ERM" (McCarthy, 1999, p. 6). Although the role, positive or negative, that social partnership has played in the recent success of the Irish economy has been debated among academics (see Kennelly and Collins, 1999, for an overview of this debate), the general consensus among those involved in the partnership process is that it has been very important and beneficial. The aim of social partnership goes beyond the desire to improve economic performance, but includes also concern for social issues. As the NCC states, "Fostering a genuine sense of social cohesion must be central" to all efforts to promote competitiveness (p. 4). The NESC, in the Introduction to their report, *Opportunities, Challenges and Capacities for Choice* (1999), also emphasises the critical role of social partnership, listing as one of its goals the desire to create a "social partnership ethos" to permeate all public policy. The most prominent manner in which social partnership has been implemented in Ireland is in the national wage agreement negotiations, but this certainly does not exhaust the possibilities of social partnership. In fact, many European countries are closely studying the Irish experience and seeing how they can emulate its high level of social co-operation.

The NCC has divided the social partnership factors into four sub-categories of indicators: General Performance; Employment and Unemployment; Health and Equality; and Crime and Social Problems. Below we will examine each factor and investigate the implications of a Basic Income system on each.

General Performance

Under the General Performance sub-category of indicators, the NCC includes: Real GDP growth; tax as a percentage of GDP; government spending; GDP per capita, and income inequality ratio. Real GDP growth and GDP per capita are both standard measures of the performance of an economy and indirectly of its competitiveness. Ireland's rate of growth in real GDP has led the developed world for all three years in which the NCC has produced reports, and has been discussed above. Like all economic statistics, it does not measure directly the economic health of the country, nor its social and economic well-being, but instead measures the level of economic transactions under the assumption that each transaction reflects an improvement in the well-being of both the buyer (the utility experienced by the consumer) and the seller (income and profits earned). Certainly this is often the case, but sadly it is not always the case (see Clark and Kavanagh, 1996a). Gross Domestic Product is a demand-determined variable, and it has been well known since Keynes published *The General Theory of Employment, Interest and Money* (1936) that demand is inversely affected by the level of income inequality (more inequality, less aggregate demand and more volatile aggregate demand; less income inequality, more aggregate demand). As our proposed Basic Income system generates a decrease in income inequality (this is shown in Chapter 6), it will necessarily lead to an increase in GDP and GDP per capita.

The effect of the percentage of GDP that is collected by the government, regardless of how it is used, is a contested issue in economics. Recent research suggests that it is not a very important factor in explaining relative growth rates, especially within the ranges that have existed in Europe over the past half-century. Thus, Ireland placing third for this indicator might not be very relevant. However, our proposal would not lead to a dramatic increase in this statistic. As we see in Table 4.3, Ireland's ranking in taxes as a per cent of GDP would increase from third to fourth. Thus a Basic Income system like the one outlined in Chapter 3 would have only a marginal effect on this indicator. Moreover, Ireland remains under the OECD average and well under the European Union and Euro Area averages. The belief that low taxes promote economic growth is more ideological than empirical, and although it is backed up by the authority of Adam Smith (writing in 1776), it is not supported by the authority of experience. In any case, when combined with the sources of government revenue that are not projected to change, a tax as a percentage of GDP of under 35 per cent would not change Ireland's relative position.

Similarly, the issue of Government spending is ambiguous in relation to the issue of competitiveness (much more significant is how the money is spent). In any case, our Basic Income system would raise government spending as a percentage of GDP from the projected 27.6 per cent for 2001 (OECD, June 2000) to 34.5 per cent, moving Ireland from second to sixth in the rankings of lowest Government spending as a share of GDP in the OECD, well below the EU average of 44.6 per cent, and the Euro Area level of 45.1 per cent. Even the most ardent proponent of *laissez-faire* would have to conclude that the proposal under consideration here would not have a meaningful impact on this indicator. The situation is much different for the income inequality ratio. As we see in Chapter 6 of this study, our Basic Income proposal reduces inequality and reduces poverty, both of which are necessary to promote social cohesion, partnership and long-term competitiveness.

Table 4.3: Taxes as a Percentage of GDP, OECD Est. 2001

Rank	Country	% of Nominal GDP	Rank	Country	% of Nominal GDP
23	Denmark	56.9	11	Czech Republic	40.5
22	Sweden	56.7	10	United Kingdom	40.4
21	Norway	52.0	9	New Zealand	40.4
20	France	49.1	8	Hungary	39.4
19	Finland	47.2	7	Poland	38.5
18	Belgium	46.8	6	Spain	37.2
17	Austria	46.6		OECD	36.5
16	Portugal	45.5	(5)	**Ireland with BI**	**34.9***
15	Italy	45.3	5 (4)	Iceland	34.5
	Euro Area	44.1	4 (3)	Australia	32.3
	European Union	44.1	3	**Ireland without BI**	32.2
14	Germany	42.4	2	Japan	31.9
13	Greece	41.8	1	USA	31.1
12	Canada	41.2			

Source: *OECD Economic Outlook*, June 2000 and Author's calculation.
*See Appendix 4.1.

Employment and Unemployment

Like growth in GDP, changes in unemployment have already been discussed in this study, and will again be discussed in the next chapter. The employment indicators listed by the NCC are: Cumulative Employment Growth; Share of General Government in Total Employment; Standardised Unemployment Rate; Level of Youth Unemployment; Long-term Unemployment; and Days Lost in Industrial Disputes. To the extent that a Basic Income policy increases aggregate demand, it will help increase the demand for workers, thus promoting employment growth (although here we are looking only at the demand side; supply-side factors will be discussed partially below, and in more detail in Chapter 5). As our Basic Income proposal includes a reduction in the administration of Social Welfare, it will lead to a small reduction in the number of government workers, though it must be admitted that this reduction will be very small and is not likely to have an impact (it should be mentioned that, as with Government spending as a percent of GDP, the Share of General Government in total employment is misleading, as what is important is what these workers are doing).

How a Basic Income policy will influence industrial relations is difficult to surmise in the context of this study, as the factors that make up this issue go well beyond the economic factors currently under consideration. One of the primary aims of the "social partnership" model is to reduce the costs that arise from the all-or-nothing approach to worker/employer relations and allow workers and employers to co-operate more with each other to achieve common goals. An argument can be made that the provision of a minimum guaranteed income would make workers more militant and thus more willing to strike (the cost of striking in terms of lost income being reduced as a percentage of their total income). However, a Basic Income would make work a much more voluntary act, based on free choice and not the condign power of material need. This could completely change the worker/employer relationship, making it more of a partnership and less based on the "confrontational" model of labour relations. Certainly, the factors that determine labour/management relations are complex, and it is likely that tax and social welfare policy are not important determinants one way or the other in generating industrial disputes. The other indicators deal with unemployment, which is discussed more fully in the next chapter.

Health and Equality

The health and equality sub-category of the NCC analysis centres on the role of women in Irish society, and secondarily on health expenditures. We will consider the second topic first. It should be obvious why the health of a nation would impact on competitiveness, though it is less obvious why total expenditures on health would be the main indicator. The treatment of total expenditures on health as an indicator illustrates one of the unavoidable limitations of the multiple indicators approach taken by the NCC report. On the one hand, a low level of government expenditures as a percentage of GDP and low labour costs are seen as good for competitiveness, while a low level of health expenditures, partly a cause of both low labour costs and low levels of government spending, is seen as adverse to competitiveness. The NCC is correct to note the importance of the health of the nation as a factor of competitiveness, and although a Basic Income system does not change the level of health spending, it should improve the health of the nation. As Richard G. Wilkinson has shown in his classic study *Unhealthy Societies: The Afflictions of Inequality* (1996), countries with the best health are the ones that have the smallest income differentials between rich and poor. Egalitarian societies have stronger community life, stronger social fabric, lower crime rates, less stress and other "corrosive effects of inequality". The New Jersey Negative Income Tax Experiments in the 1970s, which were designed to see if a guaranteed income policy would reduce labour participation, showed that many social and health variables, such as birth weight, improved significantly. We would expect similar benefits to Ireland if a Basic Income system were implemented.

The issue of how gender equity influences competitiveness has not been adequately explored and is worth a brief discussion. Gender equity frequently refers to the treatment of women, usually by the state and in the economy. The exclusion of women from various roles in society often has a negative effect on economic growth for two reasons: 1) it reduces the supply of labour and 2) it substitutes less competent men for more competent women. (Assuming equal access to employment, and perfect labour mobility, the inclusion of women into the labour force means that the more competent women will replace the less competent men.) As with all economic questions, economic growth is not a good in and of itself, but is a means to an end — higher quality of life. Calls to promote higher growth by increasing the size of the labour force (usually through higher participation rates) must be looked at in light of the overall goals and values of Irish society. Certainly, Ireland wants to promote a society where all have equal access to all forms of social participation, including, but not limited to, paid employment. We should never conclude that paid employment is necessarily more valuable or important than other forms of social participation. The parent who stays home and cares for children, and manages the household (what is often called household production), certainly contributes more than many forms of paid employment to society's well-being and future prosperity. Participation in the paid workforce should be based on a voluntary choice, not by the force of material deprivation. The experience of the US is particularly enlightening in this regard. Over the past 30 years, America has gone from one worker per household as the norm, to two full-time workers per household as the norm. This was a response to many factors, not the least of which was declining real wages and incomes that forced families to offer more labour hours per household to keep them from sliding down the economic ladder. Thus, to have a middle-class standard of living requires almost twice as much work (which means significantly less time for everything else), greatly contributing to the rise of various social problems. Ireland can produce more economic growth by forcing every adult to work full-time, but is that the type of society Ireland wants? One of the benefits of the "new economy" should be that households would have to work less, not more. A Basic Income allows both men and women more freedom in making the choices of how they wish to participate in society, using the criteria of where they feel they can make a contribution and where they feel the need is greatest, and not merely avoiding destitution.

The gender implications of introducing a Basic Income are many and varied. While our proposed Basic Income system would not impact on the gender equity factors included as indicators of competitiveness (seats held in parliament by women; administrators and managers (per cent women) and earned income share (per cent to women)), it would impact the level of equity within the household. A Basic Income policy treats both spouses equally in terms of level of payments and access to payments (since it is universal, all will get it).

It is beyond the scope of this study to review all the ways that the current social welfare system is unfair to women. We will instead review what aspects would be affected by the introduction of a Basic Income system. The Basic Income system under consideration in this study would be a clear benefit to women who are currently part of the social welfare system. These benefits come from the structural effects of moving to a universal system. Under the current system, the benefit level paid to "adult dependents" is about 60 per cent of the benefit level paid to the recipients. To give an example: under the current system, a person on unemployment benefit in 2001 would receive €108.56 per week, while the adult dependant (mostly women) in the household would receive €68.57 (or 63.2 per cent). Under a Basic Income system, they would both receive equal amounts. This is one of the most significant aspects of the structural effects of a Basic Income system. As of 1998, there were 120,136 people receiving benefits as adult dependants. A breakdown of this total can be seen in Table 4.4.

Table 4.4: Adult Dependency by Type of Payment, 1998

Type of Payment	Adult Dependants
Old Age	50,394
Illness, Disability and Caring	22,715
Unemployment Support	43,795
Misc. Benefits and Allowances	3,232
Total	120,136

A Basic Income system would also affect the labour status of partners in a relationship vis-à-vis training and other labour market initiatives. At present, in order for people who are classified as dependent to qualify for certain labour market initiatives (e.g. Community Employment Schemes) they must sign the unemployment payments over into the other's names or split the payments so that both receive half the social welfare payments. Many of the people in this situation are women. By abolishing labour market status as a requirement for benefits, a Basic Income system would enable them to apply for labour market initiatives in their own right. Many couples are currently reluctant to split their payments or to swap them as this is often seen as a sign of domestic problems. A system of individualised payments would entitle both partners to apply for places on such schemes on an equal footing. It would also provide a far simpler and more transparent means of accessing labour market initiatives. This would be the case because entitlements would be far more transparent and uncertainty regarding benefits would be reduced.

Home Duties

One of the great injustices of the present economic system is the fact that some activities are rewarded by society with a wage while other activities, which often are as important (and in many cases more important) to the economic and social health of the nation, are not rewarded. This is particularly the case for those in home duties. A Basic Income helps to support those households where one chooses to stay out of the paid workforce to instead work at home. This group accounts for the largest percentage of females over 15 in Ireland (based on the 1996 census). A Basic Income clearly benefits these individuals, as they now have an independent source of income.

There would also be an impact on the status of individuals who would no longer be assessed as dependent on another. A system of universal payments would radically alter the distribution of income within some households. Assessing the total income of a household can often be a misleading indicator of the distribution of income within that household. If one party within the household has power over the distribution within the household, then he or she can determine the level of income of the others to a large extent. A system of universal payments that ensures that everyone is guaranteed access to a minimum income provides a safety net for partners who are denied an equitable share of the household's resources. It should be emphasised that a Basic Income would not completely rectify the imbalance within households; however, it would provide people with a guaranteed source of independent income.

Crime and Social Problems

The last sub-category of the social partnership section of indicators of competitiveness is "crime and social problems". Crime and social problems have a damaging effect on competitiveness for two reasons. First and foremost, those involved in crime and those who are overwhelmed by the various social ills of our times are not flourishing to the best of their abilities, neither promoting their own happiness nor contributing to the common good. Ireland's greatest resource has always been its people, and for Ireland to create a truly great society it will need the contributions of the entire population. It cannot afford to leave anyone out. Social exclusion costs both the individuals excluded and society as a whole (in lost contributions). Secondly, crime and other social problems have a double cost to society, as they divert valuable resources (both human and non-human) away from activities that promote social well-being and real economic progress towards dealing with the effects of social exclusion. Ironically, crime and social problems tend to contribute to many of the economic indicators we use to measure economic and social progress, especially those that rely solely on market transactions. The social decay that is caused by the over-commercialisation of society, and the replacing of social values with material values, inevitably lead to higher levels of market transactions. Higher crime, juvenile delinquency and the associated property damage, the breakup of families, all increase the demand for goods and services from the market economy. Two of the biggest factors in the growth of GDP in the US over the past two decades have been crime and the breakup of the family (the leading cause of social problems), both of which generate a great deal of market activity (Cobb, Halstead and Rowe, 1995). As a Basic Income system reduces some of the barriers to social participation (poverty and employment traps) it will have a positive effect on crime and social problems. But more importantly, a Basic Income system has the potential of ending material poverty. The Government agencies that currently "serve" the poor in fact, because of the means-testing of benefits, end up "regulating" the poor. The relationship between these government agencies and the poor has the potential to be radically changed under a Basic Income system, and these institutions can return to the goals and ideals that prompted their creation, to helping people deal with life's difficulties and challenges. Lastly, one important aspect of a great society is that all participate. Social participation is a good in and of itself.

People

The second of the seven major categories of indicators of competitiveness in the NCC Annual Competitiveness Report for 2000 is simply titled People. By people, the NCC seems to mean the quality of the Irish labour force, their levels of skill and their incentives to work. The indicators in this section are broken down into four sub-categories: Primary and Secondary Education; Tertiary Education; Work Incentives; and Labour Market. While a Basic Income policy would have little impact on primary and secondary education (with the exception that it would allow parents more time to participate in their children's education), it will impact tertiary education, which we discuss below. Work incentives and labour market factors are discussed in the next chapter.

Tertiary Education

Higher education and lifelong learning are very important for the new economy and one of the projected flexibilities that the new labour markets will need is the ability for workers to continue to improve their human capital (acquire new skills and training). Traditionally, once students have finished their higher education they received their diploma and were mostly done with their formal education (although it should be noted that many of the professions have long required continuous education in some form or another, and that most occupations provide most of the necessary skills through job experience). The new model is for moving between paid employment and further education. A Basic Income supports this new labour market. Workers who want to be retrained, either in their present field, or changing fields, would have the Basic Income payment to live on while they are earning less or no income. Furthermore, a Basic Income makes it easier for low-income households to send their children to tertiary education, as they will not need the income these teenagers and young adults would have contributed to the households.

BASIC INCOME AND FUTURE PROSPERITY

Future prosperity in Ireland depends on a continuation of the trends that have promoted the current situation. On the macroeconomic side, this means Irish labour costs must be substantially lower than their competitors. As Irish productivity statistics are greatly exaggerated, due to the extensive use of transfer pricing by multinationals operating in Ireland, we cannot assume that the statistical convergence that has been noted in terms of productivity and per capita incomes means that Ireland can compete with Europe and the US on an equal cost of labour basis. Yet the policy of trading tax concessions for wage increases is not one that can last long, as such a bargain makes the rising income inequality situation even worse (tax cuts disproportionately benefit the more affluent and completely miss lower income households). Some system of sharing the benefits of this new economic progress more equally must be found, and a Basic Income system would work towards this end.

While rising investment levels, mostly from overseas, and rising exports explain much of Ireland's recent economic success, they are only part of the story; in order for these factors to have had such an impact, there had to be the right environment. The existence of a large pool of highly skilled labour is certainly a precondition for the high levels of foreign investment, as is the existence of wage moderation. The rise in what economists call "human capital" thus plays an important role in Ireland's economic success; but an equally important role can be ascribed to the rise of what has been called "social capital". The clearest example of this in terms of Ireland's economy is the efforts of the various national wage agreements and of the social partners to consider the interests of all sectors of Irish society. The most direct benefit of the national wage agreements has been moderation in wage growth, which has made Irish labour more attractive relative to European labour in general. But this is only part of the bargain, and if we have only this part then Irish prosperity will be short-lived. Employed Irish workers have traded higher wage growth for higher levels of employment growth, substituting lower tax rates for higher wages. As we see in Chapter 6, this has generated a rise in income inequality, and will, unless the other half of the bargain is accomplished, lead to greater tensions in Irish society. The future success of the Irish economy will depend on its ability to promote flexibility in a way that also promotes social cohesion and ensures that all reap the fruits of economic progress. Without the commitment to social inclusion and equity, the new economy will end up being merely the creation of wealth for the few by transferring the costs of the new economy to the many.

Appendix 4.1

Calculation of Taxes as a Percentage of GDP, 2001

According to Budget 2000, the projected tax revenues for 2001 were €27,629.50 million. Under our proposed Basic Income system, the income tax is eliminated, reducing €8,484.39 million from this number, leaving €19,145.11 in tax revenue plus €493.93 million in non-tax revenue. Our proposal adds €2,289.34 million (Social Responsibility Tax) and €18,616.90 million, giving a total tax take of €40,545.28. The ESRI forecasts GDP at market prices to be €116,033.74 million in 2001. This gives a "taxes as a percentage of GDP" ratio of 40,545.28/ 116,033.74. Even if we use the GNP measure, this would raise the percentage of the economy going to taxes to 41.5 per cent, well below the Euro Area and European Union averages. This is, however, adjusting for the discrepancies between GDP and GNP in Ireland and not in other European countries, a good number of which have similar discrepancies.

Chapter 5

CHANGING LABOUR MARKETS: TOWARDS REAL FLEXIBILITY

THE CHANGING NATURE OF WORK

As with the last "great transformation", the transition to the new economy of the 21st century promises to create profound changes in the organisation of work, families and communities (Carnoy, 2000). The forces of technological change and globalisation have the potential to increase the quality of life and help Ireland and the world build truly great societies. However, they also have the potential to transform societies and economies into segmented communities of haves and have-nots, increasing the level of polarisation that has been created by the "old economy". Any economic transformation will have both costs and benefits and it is important that both costs and benefits be included in any analysis of the "new economy". Too often, we can get swept up in the high-tech hype and only emphasise the marvels of technological change and world trade without fully accounting for the new costs created by the same processes that have generated this new material prosperity.

In this chapter, we will concentrate on the changes in work, but it is beneficial to look briefly at how the new economy will impact families and communities as well. Too often, work is understood purely from a narrow "economic" perspective, including in our analysis only the factors that directly influence the supply and demand for labour, the determination of wages and the level of employment. Yet the full costs and benefits to work go beyond the wages paid to workers and the contributions to output and profits received by employers. The full cost of a worker includes many family and social costs. Workers need supportive families and communities in order to be productive. Families provide not only the social support for labour market participation, they also produce and socialise the next generation of workers. Similarly, communities are necessary for productive workers, both today (creating a safe environment for economic activity) and for tomorrow (educating future workers). Yet the new economy places greater stress on families and communities. It creates a more individualised economic space, weakening the social bonds of community. It also calls for greater labour market flexibility, which often translates into greater insecurity for workers, more atypical forms of employment and greater claims on the time of workers. Along with the potential for widening the gulf between the haves and the have-nots, the most serious challenge the new economy is creating is in how we provide for the economic and social security which a good society demands while at the same time providing for the flexibility which the new economy requires.

CHANGES IN WORK

Beyond the trite speeches on how "brain power" will replace "mechanical" or physical power is the reality that the new economy will bring about significant changes in the work life of many groups in society, changes which will be as dramatic as those brought about by the rise of the factory system in the early 19th century. Many of these changes revolve around the issue of labour adapting to the new technology and lifelong learning, both issues of labour flexibility. Another unavoidable aspect of the new economy is the decline in the "job for life" goal of the Keynes-Beveridge model and the increasingly temporary and short-lived nature of employment relations. On the macro level, this is seen in the secular trend upwards in the level of unemployment in the advanced capitalist economies. At the micro level, we see this in the rise in "atypical employment". The key labour market issue of this new century is to find mechanisms for accommodating the flexibility needs of the new economy while supporting the position of the worker in an environment of high capital mobility and insuring that the benefits of economic progress are shared by all. In Chapter 2, we looked at the macro issues of rising unemployment and technological change, and in Chapter 4 we examined how to be competitive in this new environment. The various factors that have promoted the competitiveness of the Irish economy in the new economy centre on cost competitiveness. This cost competitiveness has greatly promoted exports and foreign direct investment, both of which are the driving forces behind the "Celtic Tiger" economy.

In this chapter, we look at some of the micro labour issues, specifically the importance of labour flexibility and the rise in "atypical employment". We will then look at how a Basic Income policy would influence labour supply and demand. One of the central focuses of much of the labour market research in the past decade, in Ireland and the OECD in general, has been the influence of social insurance on labour market outcomes. Thus, in examining how our proposed Basic Income system will influence the labour market in Ireland, we examine these issues, especially the two topics of the "tax wedge" and "replacement ratios". Finally, we return to the topic of Chapter 4 with an examination of how a Basic Income proposal will affect the competitiveness of the Irish economy vis-à-vis its influence on the labour market, taking the National Competitiveness Council's recent Annual Competitiveness Report as our guide.

LABOUR MARKET FLEXIBILITY

> An intriguing aspect of the recent wave of productivity acceleration is that US businesses and workers appear to have benefited more from the recent advances in information technology than their counterparts in Europe or Japan. Those countries, of course, have also participated in this

wave of invention and innovation, but they appear to have been slower to exploit it. The relatively inflexible and, hence, more costly labor markets of these economies appear to be a significant part of the explanation. The elevated rates of return offered by the newer technologies in the United States are largely the result of a reduction in labor costs per unit of output. The rates of return on investment in the same new technologies are correspondingly less in Europe and Japan because businesses there face higher costs of displacing workers than we do. Here, labor displacement is more readily countenanced both by law and by culture. Parenthetically, because our costs of dismissing workers are lower, the potential costs of hiring and the risks associated with expanding employment are less. The result of this significantly higher capacity for job dismissal has been, counterintuitively, a dramatic decline in the US unemployment rate in recent years. (Alan Greenspan, speech to National Governor's Association, 11 July 2000)

One of the key factors mentioned in all discussions of the new economy is labour market flexibility. In many ways, labour market flexibility is a double-edged sword, especially in the context of the Keynes-Beveridge welfare state. Labour market flexibility, or at least some aspects of labour market flexibility, is a necessary precondition for competing in the new economy. However, it is only though the regulation of labour markets — that is, by creating rigidities — that advanced capitalist economies have been able to increase the living standards of the majority of the population and ensure that the benefits of economic progress are more equitably shared. Thus, what worked in the past is no longer an option. New methods of promoting competitiveness (the subject of the last chapter) and equity (the subject of the next chapter) are needed. This chapter, therefore, will serve as a bridge between Chapters 4 (competitiveness) and 6 (poverty and income inequality). Both issues, which roughly make up much of the equity/efficiency focus of this book, are greatly affected by developments in the labour market. Future competitiveness hinges, at least partly, on the ability of Irish workers and companies to adjust to changes in

Changing Labour Markets

market conditions. However, much of the rise in income inequality also stems from developments in labour markets, and under the current "rules of the game" the factors that promote flexibility, and thus competitiveness, also promote income inequality and higher levels of poverty. The attraction of a Basic Income system is its promise of allowing Ireland to promote both efficiency and equity, to promote greater levels of competitiveness and allow all to share in the benefits of this economic progress.

Types of Flexibility

Labour market flexibility is a phrase that is generally used with a positive connotation; it is not often that we hear someone come out against it, at least in principle. Often the term is a buzzword, meaning different things to different constituencies. However, one thing is certain: when one group asks another to be more flexible, they are seeking some concessions. Thus the call for greater labour market flexibility by businesses is a call for greater power over the production process by capital. It can be argued that the new economy requires this redistribution of control. What is more certain is the fact that the increase in the mobility of capital and other factors of globalisation have given them the ability to demand such control. But we should not forget that workers and citizens, and society as a whole, are being asked to give up some of their power and influence. Some form of institutional adjustment will have to be made to ensure that this transfer of power does not also generate a shifting of risk and uncertainty to workers and the poor, making labour market flexibility merely labour market insecurity.

There are essentially four types of labour market flexibility we will consider here: labour costs, adaptability, mobility and work time and scheduling. When economists write about labour market flexibility, especially as it relates to unemployment, their conception is almost exclusively in terms of labour costs, specifically wage flexibility. The idea here is that when the demand for workers falls, rather than there being an increase in unemployment, wages would fall (thus you have price effects instead of quantity effects). This pre-Keynesian notion assumes that if wage flexibility exists, there could never be mass unemployment. Keynes and the Great Depression showed how inaccurate this theory and policy proposal was, and common sense tells us that wage flexibility is a bad idea. Just imagine the level of uncertainty in the economy if all workers' wages rose and fell with changes in market conditions (like stock or commodity prices). There is considerable evidence that wage flexibility is increasing (Standing, 1999). Some of this can be seen in the rise in wage inequality (caused by changes in relative real wages). Other aspects can be seen with the increased use of time-rate and piece-rate pay instead of a fixed wage, and in the increased use of incentive pay (stock options as an example) and profit sharing (ibid., p. 95).

But labour cost flexibility is more than wage flexibility. Labour costs are determined by many factors (ibid., pp. 98–101): overhead costs, fiscal costs (paid to government), training costs, protection costs (worker, consumer and community safety), labour turnover costs, motivational costs, productivity costs, adaptability costs and bureaucratic behaviour costs. At least some part of the decline in labour costs in Ireland (see Chapter 4), and in other OECD countries, stems from a shifting of some of these costs from the firms to the workers or to society. To give an example, the educational system subsidises business training costs to a large extent, and the more the educational system is adjusted to being a source of trained workers, the greater this subsidy becomes. Social insurance, as we see below, pays for a large share of the protection costs of production in Ireland. A Basic Income can be seen as compensation for the shifting of costs. The benefits of flexible labour costs generally go to the firm. Part of this benefit is the ability to make adjustments to new market conditions, but part of this is merely a shift in the costs of production away from the firm and onto the worker, consumers and society as a whole, simply because they have the power to do so. This sort of labour market flexibility is neither good for society nor necessary for the technological aspects of the new economy, but it is brought about by the increased capital mobility of globalisation and thus is a reality that must be dealt with.

The other forms of labour market flexibility — adaptability, mobility and work time and scheduling — have all become important ingredients in the new economy and are, in many ways, the result of the need for flexible production in order to be competitive. However, they too can amount to a shift in costs away from the firm and towards workers and society unless some system is created in order to reduce the risk and uncertainty of workers and citizens and to ensure that all benefit from the new technology. In order for the benefits of these new flexibilities to be realised in a way that benefits all, some system of reducing these new insecurities will be necessary. Increased mobility means that workers will be expected to move between jobs more often, yet they have to be supported all the time, even when they are between jobs. A Basic Income does this. A more adaptable workforce means that employers will need fewer total workers, yet those that will be made redundant will need to be supported. A Basic Income does this. Flexibility in hours and schedules means that more workers will be "atypical workers", which is discussed below. But these people need to be supported full-time, and a Basic Income does this.

CHANGES IN EMPLOYMENT

The new economy requires flexibilities that were not necessary for the mass production "Fordist" economy of the 20th century. One way that these flexibilities have become institutionalised in the Irish economy, as well as in other OECD countries, is the rise in what has been called "atypical employment", or "non-standard forms of employment". The most common forms of "atypical employment" are part-time work, temporary or casual work, consultants, sub-contractors, agency workers, home workers, teleworkers and concealed workers.[1]

Atypical work is commonly associated with weaker labour market position. The extent to which this is the case depends largely on the social policies of a country as a whole. From the point of view of the well-being of an individual, it is also crucial whether part-time or temporary work is voluntary or involuntary; in other words, whether flexibility serves primarily the needs of the employer or the worker (Nurmi, 1999).

In looking at "atypical" forms of employment, we should keep in mind both the positive and negative aspects, as well as the realities of the flexibilities of the new economy and, most importantly, the well-being of the worker. On the positive side, "atypical" employment can help individuals enter the labour force and it can allow the individual free time to pursue other interests and to fulfil family responsibilities. However, "atypical" employment is frequently at low pay, without benefits, does not meet the requirements of social insurance programmes and is often involuntary (the worker would prefer full-time work).

Part-Time Work

One of the most dramatic changes in the Irish labour market has been the growth in part-time work. As we see in Table 5.1, part-time work has more than doubled in the last decade, and while most of the part-time workers have been female, the upward trend for male workers was higher than for females.

Table 5.1: Incidence of Part-Time Working in Ireland, 1983–97 (ILO basis)

Year	Men %	Women %	All %
1983	2.7	15.6	6.7
1990	3.4	17.6	8.1
1993	4.8	21.3	10.8
1994	5.1	21.7	11.3
1995	5.4	23.1	12.1
1996	5.0	22.1	11.6
1997	5.4	23.1	12.3
1998	7.8	30.1	16.7

Source: *Eurostat Labour Force Survey*, and CSO, from O'Connell (1999).

In 1997, about 20 per cent of the part-time female workers were part-time because they could not find full-time work, while the rate for male workers was considerably higher at just under 50 per cent (falling from nearly 60 per cent in 1995) (Nurmi, 1999). Part-time work is beneficial to the worker when it is the result of a voluntary choice, but it is a sign of weakness in the labour market when it is involuntary. However, what we need to know is why part-time workers want to work full-time. If it is because the income earned part-time is insufficient, then a Basic Income would certainly make part-time work more appealing.

Temporary Work

The advantages of temporary work for employers is obvious, as it gives them "numerical" flexibility; that is, they can adjust their labour force easily to changes in the demand for their products. This shifts all of the "demand risk" onto the workers and away from employers. The extent of temporary work in Ireland is about equal to the European average, fluctuating for males between 6 per cent and 8 per cent, and for females between 11 per cent and 13 per cent, from 1993 to 1997 (Nurmi, 1999). (Spain has by far the highest level of temporary workers in Europe at around 35 per cent.) As of 1997, about half of the females engaged in temporary work in Ireland, and over 60 per cent of the male workers, were temporary because of an inability to find full-time employment (ibid.). Just over 10 per cent of the temporary male workers in 1997 would not take up full employment, while 30 per cent of the females chose temporary employment voluntarily. While there is certainly a good deal of overlap between part-time and temporary workers, it is clear that as Ireland increases its role in the global economy, its work force must be competitive with other export-driven economies, and this includes labour flexibility.

BASIC INCOME AND WORK INCENTIVES

Much of the research on labour markets focuses on the influence of social welfare and social insurance on the decision of workers to take up a job. This approach is very one-sided, because it looks at the "costs" of social welfare and insurance without looking at the significant benefits and necessary role it plays in the efficient operation of the economy and society. Before we look at how a Basic Income system would impact the labour market, it is important to look at this issue fully. Thus, we will first discuss the necessary role of social insurance and social welfare. Here we will see that it is part of what could be called the social overhead costs of economic activity. Then we will examine the two statistics economists have concentrated on when examining the impact of social insurance and welfare on labour market activity: replacement ratios and the tax wedge.

The argument that social insurance creates a disincentive to work rests on the contention that workers will be less likely to take up a job if the net benefits of the job (after-tax income) is not sufficiently greater than the benefit levels provided by social insurance. Thus, the replacement ratio is seen as reducing the willingness of workers to take job offers. Given all the attention it has gotten in Irish studies of labour issues, and especially the topic of Basic Income and the labour market (this is the bulk of the TWIG (Expert Working Group on the Integration of the Tax and Social Welfare Systems) report analysis of labour market issues), it is surprising how little empirical evidence has been offered to support replacement ratios as a meaningful statistic. Furthermore, the main conclusion of this literature, implicitly and explicitly, is that the way to reduce the replacement ratio is by reducing social welfare benefits and not by increasing the net pay of work. The problem is not that social welfare benefits are too generous, it is that they are not universal, and that when a person takes up a job they face high marginal tax and lost benefit rates (that is, when you add the taxes paid plus the benefits lost due to taking up the job), which can act as a disincentive for taking up a job. Lastly, almost completely ignored in this literature are the benefits of social insurance in supporting the labour market. These benefits are worth noting here, as anything that replaces the current system of social welfare will need to provide the same beneficial effects.

Benefits of Social Insurance

A report by the Department of Social Welfare (1996) highlighted the important role social insurance plays in supporting the labour market. First, they note that social insurance is only one aspect of labour competitiveness:

> 5.1.9 When assessing the impact of labour costs on competitiveness, it should be borne in mind that Social Insurance costs are only one element of labour costs and must be considered in the context of other statutory charges, especially income tax. Specifically in relation to Social Insurance, the system involves benefits as well as costs and both must be taken into account when considering the impact of Social Insurance on the competitiveness of business. The system provides important services such as pensions, in-work benefits and other direct and indirect labour market sup-

ports so that the benefits deriving from Social Insurance contributions — both for workers and employers — are an important ingredient of the competitiveness "mix".

5.2.1 Social Insurance payments are an important factor within the overall competitiveness mix as they provide income support to workers who fall ill or encounter other contingencies, such as retirement and redundancy. Were it not for Social Insurance employers would have to contribute to these costs through other mechanisms such as enhanced in-house sick pay and occupational pension schemes. The cost of such schemes would, as a consequence, be higher than it currently is.

Social insurance thus pays for many of the labour costs mentioned above. Clearly, both workers and employers benefit from having some form of social protection. As John Maurice Clark has demonstrated in his classic *Studies in the Economics of Overhead Costs* (1923), there is a distinction between the full costs of production and the costs that are actually paid by a business for a specific activity. For a large firm, the problem of overhead costs is well known, but the principle holds for society as a whole. The full cost of reproducing this in society and the economy has to be paid, but much of it is not compensated through regular market relations. Part of these costs is the support for workers who are unemployed, for whatever reason. Also included here are those who work in the social economy or household production. Both provide necessary work for social reproduction, yet are outside of traditional market relations. Under normal conditions, these two activities are supported by the market compensation of a household member (e.g., one parent works at a paid job and financially supports the parent who works at household production). Here part of the overhead costs of market production is the necessary household production, which, if the market is fully efficient, will be compensated through a living household wage to the worker in the market economy. Most of the people who are outside the labour force (elderly, children, adults in home duties, disabled, sick, unemployed, etc.) also fall into this category of social overhead costs, and currently social insurance and social welfare payments supplement their incomes. Thus social insurance and social welfare are necessary for any civilised society and efficient economy. The problem with the current welfare states in the advanced capitalist economies is that they do not fully cover everyone who contributes to society, or they are inefficient mechanisms for covering social overhead costs, that is, they are too costly or create barriers to fuller social participation (such as poverty or unemployment traps).

CALCULATING INCENTIVES AND DISINCENTIVES

As stated, almost all of the standard analysis of the influence of tax and social welfare benefits on labour market behaviour centres on two variables: replacement ratios and the tax wedge. In this section we estimate both statistics for our Basic Income proposal, and compare them with estimates under the current social welfare system (year 2000). After these estimates are provided we will discuss their implications for labour market participation rates in Ireland under a Basic Income system.

Tax Wedge

The tax wedge is the difference between the cost of employing a worker to the employer (wages plus contributions to social security) and the after-tax and benefit incomes of the worker (net income). Theoretically, a high tax wedge reduces employment in two ways:

1. Because it increases the cost to employers for hiring workers (employers need to pay higher incomes to match the post-tax income expectations of workers), employers will hire fewer workers (assuming a downward sloping demand curve for labour);

2. Assuming that the supply of workers is determined by the net income from work, the tax wedge reduces the income

workers get to keep (net of taxes) and thus reduces the supply of labour.

Both are suspect explanations of labour market behaviour. The negative effect of the tax wedge on an employer's decisions to hire workers assumes that this tax falls upon the employer. Yet in reality, much, if not all of it, is typically passed on to others. As the Department of Social Welfare's report on *Social Insurance in Ireland* (1996) notes:

> The Commission on Taxation concluded that the actual incidence of Employers' PRSI was diffuse as it is "partly passed on to consumers in higher prices, partly passed on to labour in the form of lower levels of income and employment and partly borne by employers through reduced profits." . . . [And that] "there is a also a growing body of empirical evidence for the claim that the incidence of (Employers' Social Insurance) falls on workers".

The influence of the tax wedge on the willingness of workers to offer their labour is also empirically weak. Firstly, the overall influence of taxes and benefit levels of labour supply, it turns out, is very small. Labour economists have long noted that tax rates and benefit levels have very little impact on adult males and single females and that only married females seem to respond significantly to changes in taxes or benefit changes. The reason is because social and cultural factors (as well as the necessity to earn money to survive, since few social welfare benefit systems provide a standard of living one would call comfortable) outweigh the logic of "rational economic man", which economists assume determines all human activity.

Secondly, the influence of something like a tax wedge on labour activity is rarely an either/or situation. No one would seriously argue that workers would drop out of the labour market because of a change in taxes or benefit levels (these never change so radically as to cause this extreme behaviour). The change, it is alleged, will come in terms of a reduction of hours worked. However, most workers do not have the power to set

Changing Labour Markets 89

how many hours they work, and rarely can adjust them in response to changes in their real net pay. Generally, only parttime and temporary workers have this flexibility (though certainly not all or even most of them have this type of power). As these two categories are dominated by married women, it is not surprising that here we do find some evidence of changes in labour supply due to changes in taxes and wages.

Lastly, an increase in taxes will have both an income and a substitution effect, and the tax wedge argument only considers the substitution effect (workers are substituting work leisure for work at the higher tax/low net income levels). Yet most evidence suggests that income effects overwhelm substitution effects in these types of situations. In fact, a look towards history quickly confirms this. A common way for the king or ruler to force the people to work harder for him is to raise their taxes.

The last comment we will make on the theoretical issue of the tax wedge is that it looks at such taxes only as a cost, and ignores the benefits of social insurance, which are likely to be much greater than the costs. What the employer seems to want, according to the proponents of the tax wedge cause of unemployment, is to be a free rider, that is, to get the benefit of having social insurance provided for their workers (which is a legitimate and real cost of production that either the employer, the worker or society must cover) without having to pay their fair share. As the evidence suggests that most of this is passed on to the consumer, that is, it is included in the cost of production, it does not seem that it would enter into the employer's calculus on hiring.

In Figures 5.1 to 5.4, we see the tax wedge for different households under the Basic Income proposal developed in Chapter 3 and under the current system (Budget 2000). Figure 5.1 looks at a household with a married couple, one income and no children. Here we see that the current tax and benefit system has tax wedges that are significantly higher than what would exist under our Basic Income proposal. Moreover, low-income households, under our Basic Income system, have a negative tax wedge, which acts like a "wage subsidy". Following the logic of the tax wedge as a disincentive, a negative tax wedge must be seen as an incentive to employment.

Figure 5.1: Tax Wedge, Married, One Income, No Children

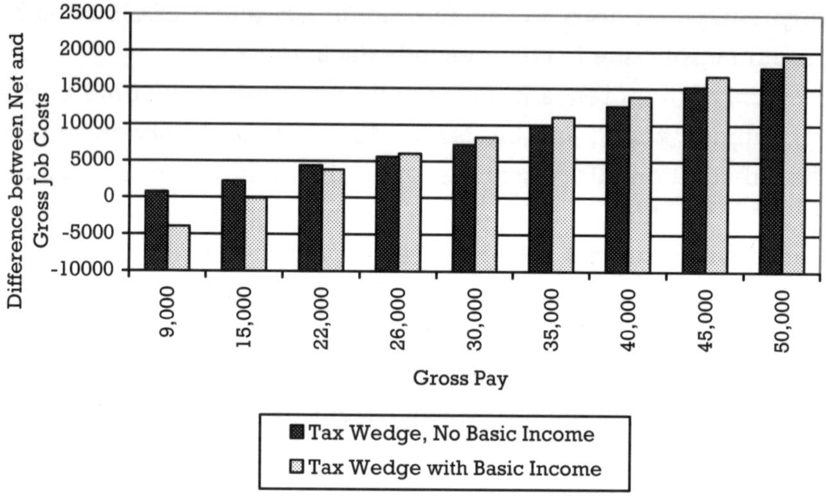

[Bar chart showing Difference between Net and Gross Job Costs (y-axis, from -10000 to 25000) versus Gross Pay (x-axis: 9,000; 15,000; 22,000; 26,000; 30,000; 35,000; 40,000; 45,000; 50,000). Legend: Tax Wedge, No Basic Income; Tax Wedge with Basic Income.]

Source: Author's calculation based on Budget 2000 Tables.

In Figure 5.2, we see the tax wedges for married couples, one income and two children. Here we see that our Basic Income proposal has higher "wage subsidies", or negative tax wedge, for low-income households and lower tax wedges for middle and high-income households.

Figure 5.3 is for married couples with two incomes and two children. Here we see the same differences between the current system and a Basic Income system.

Our final example, Figure 5.4, is the tax wedge for single households.

Changing Labour Markets 91

Figure 5.2: Tax Wedge, Married Couple, One Income, Two Children

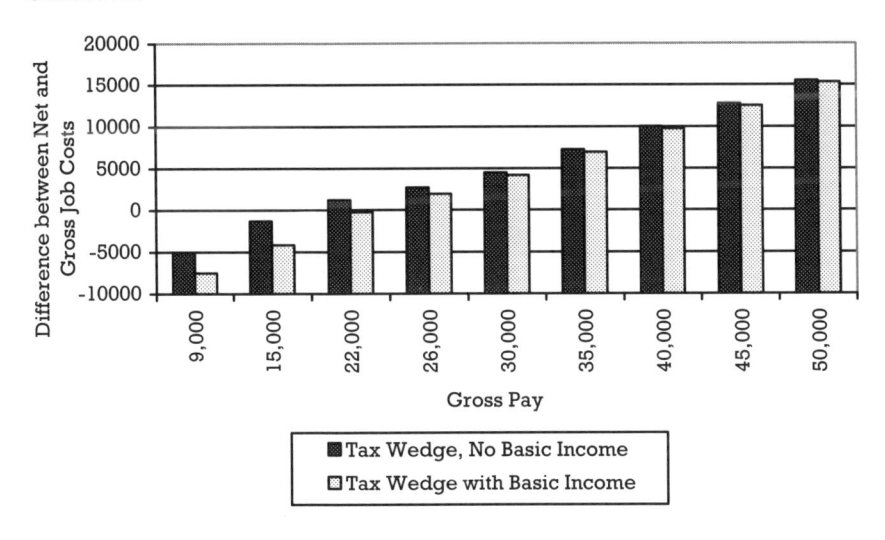

Source: Author's calculation based on Budget 2000 Tables.

Figure 5.3: Tax Wedge, Married Couple, Two Incomes, Two Children

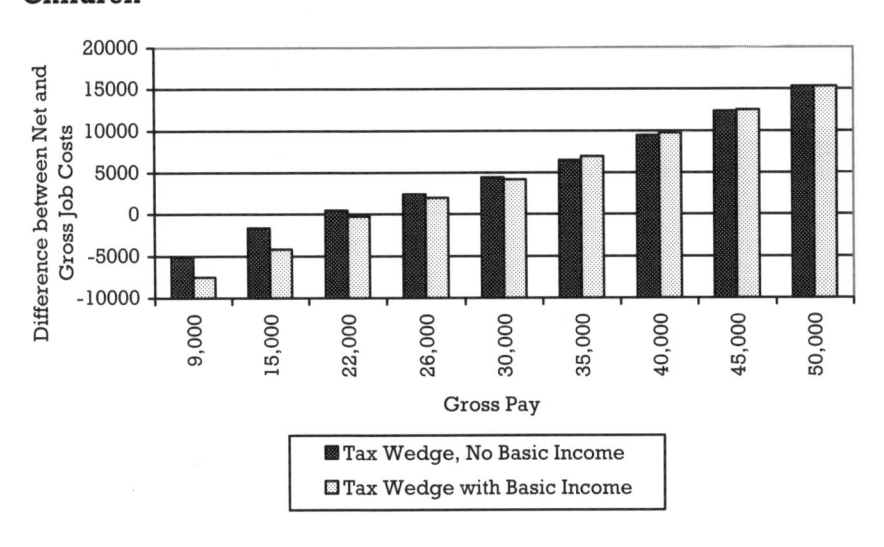

Source: Author's calculation based on Budget 2000 Tables.

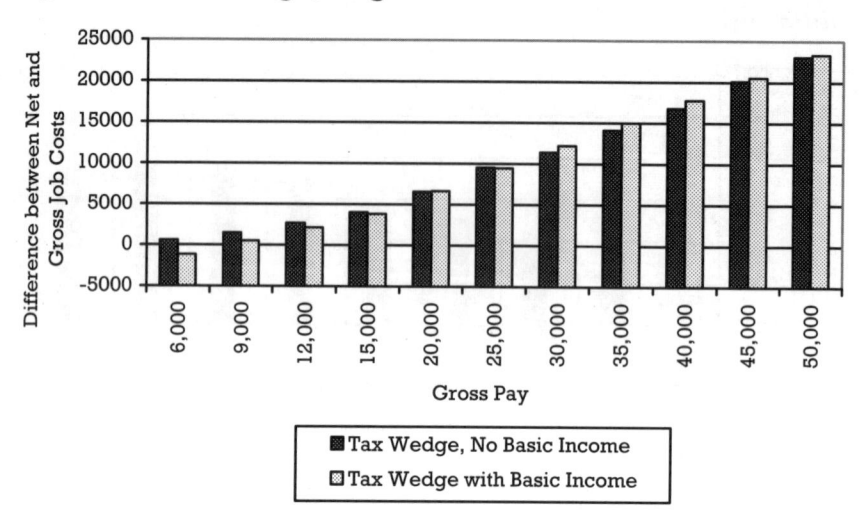

Figure 5.4: Tax Wedge, Single

[Bar chart showing Difference between Net and Gross Job Costs (y-axis, -5000 to 25000) against Gross Pay (x-axis, 6,000 to 50,000) comparing Tax Wedge, No Basic Income and Tax Wedge with Basic Income]

Source: Author's calculation based on Budget 2000 Tables.

Again we see that our Basic Income proposal outperforms the current tax and social welfare system, giving low-income households greater benefits than currently exist. In terms of tax wedge analysis, our Basic Income system is much better than the current one, providing strong incentives to take up a job.

Replacement Ratios

The argument that high replacement ratios increase unemployment is very similar to the tax wedge argument. The replacement ratio is the difference between income earned from employment and the benefits received if one were unemployed. As is argued in the TWIG Report (1996, pp. 174–175):

> Because unemployment benefits reduce the cost of becoming unemployed, employed people may take greater risks with the security of their jobs, for example in individual disputes with an employer or in collective bargaining over wages. People who feel that they are better off unemployed than in their present employment may be less willing to accept changes in wages and conditions which might be necessary to safeguard their jobs. This can have a negative

effect on employment. It can be expected that these disincentives will pose an even greater problem as increased competition arising from the globalisation of the world economy will put further cost pressure on firms competing on the margin against low-cost producers and employers seek to improve their trading conditions.

As with the tax wedge analysis, only the negative aspects of unemployment assistance are considered in most analysis of its impact on the labour market. Unemployment assistance allows those who are out of paid work to still consume goods and services (though at a lower level), supporting aggregate demand (and the jobs this spending supports) and is one of the automatic stabilisers that help to prevent small downturns and recessions from becoming crashes and depressions. Secondly, for the replacement ratio argument to make sense, there must be job vacancies to match the numbers and skills of the unemployed, and the persistence of unemployment is due to the unemployed choosing to be unemployed. As high levels of unemployment have never been accompanied by high levels of job vacancies, it seems that this explanation is a non-starter. (In fact, it is common that during periods of high unemployment, the news will report stories of employers taking hundreds of applications for a handful of jobs.) The notion that workers determine the level of employment seems to have everything backwards. Since a Basic Income is a universal programme, with the benefits not being reduced by one's employment status, the notion of replacement ratios does not make much sense. The worker who takes a job gets to keep both the wages earned (minus taxes) and the Basic Income benefit; thus they do not have to choose one over the other.

The replacement ratio (RR) is a statistic designed to measure the extent of the unemployment trap. Unemployment traps are said to exist whenever a situation exists where a person who is unemployed would not significantly improve their economic circumstances if they took up employment. In extreme cases, the unemployed person would be made worse off (that is, if one sums up all lost benefits due to working and subtracts it from their after-tax income, the person's net income is reduced by working). This creates a significant disincentive to taking up a job. "This disincentive is usually represented and measured in terms of the Replacement Ratio, i.e. the ratio of income when unemployed to the net income if employed" (TWIG, p. 13).

Using the tables provided in Budget 2000 on the impact on different households, we can calculate the replacement ratio for different household types. Here we give the replacement ratio under the current system and what would exist under our Basic Income proposal. We see that in the relevant cases, the replacement ratio is lower under our Basic Income proposal than it is under the current system. Only at very high incomes, where replacement ratios are very low and economically meaningless, do our Basic Income proposal's replacement ratios exceed those under the current system. But at the income levels where replacement ratios might matter, our Basic Income proposal produces replacement ratios that are significantly lower than the current levels. This is rather easy to explain. Since a Basic Income system is a universal programme, which does not change with changes in labour market status, that is, the Basic Income payment does not change, households do not experience drops in their non-labour income with an increase in waged income; thus the replacement ratio under a Basic Income policy is lower by raising the "net income if employed". This contrasts with the typical view of replacement ratios which calls for a reduction in the statistic by reducing benefits, i.e., making work more attractive by making being unemployed more unattractive. This Thatcher/Reagan approach is particularly punitive on the poor and low-income households, and is also not an effective means of increasing employment, which, as we have seen earlier in this study, is done at the macro level.

In Figures 5.5 to 5.8, we see that our Basic Income proposal has lower replacement ratios for all but those in high pay, and it does this by increasing the net income of those in work, instead of by reducing the incomes of those out of work.

Changing Labour Markets 95

Figure 5.5: Replacement Ratios, Single, Current and with Basic Income

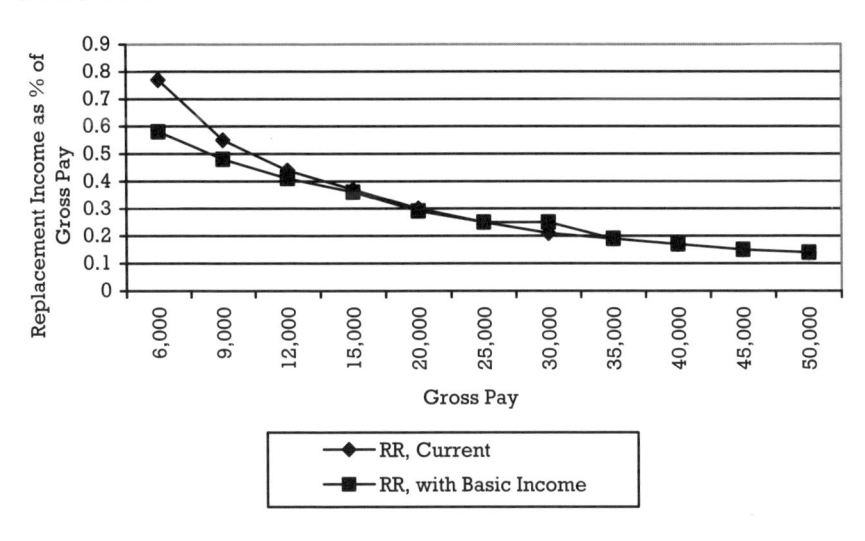

Source: Author's calculations based on Budget 2000

Figure 5.6: Replacement Ratios, Married Couple, One Income, No Children, Current and with Basic Income

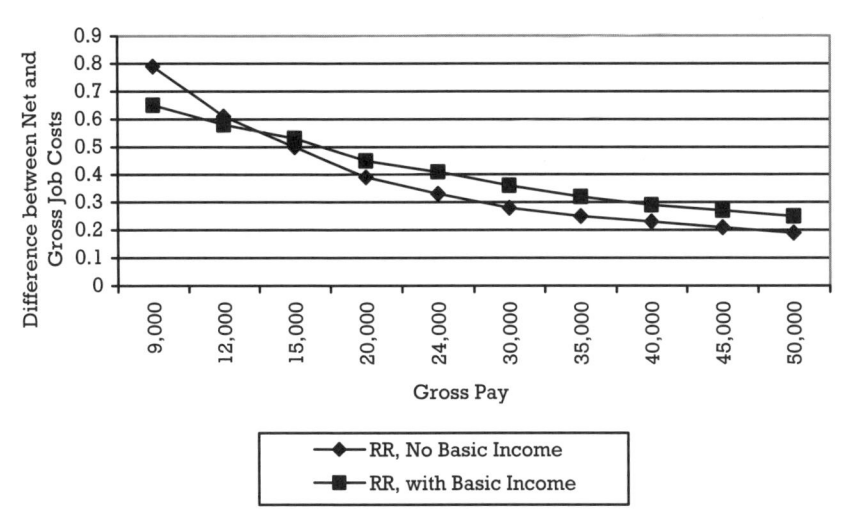

Source: Author's calculations based on Budget 2000

Figure 5.7: Replacement Ratios, Married Couple, One Income, Two Children, Current and with Basic Income

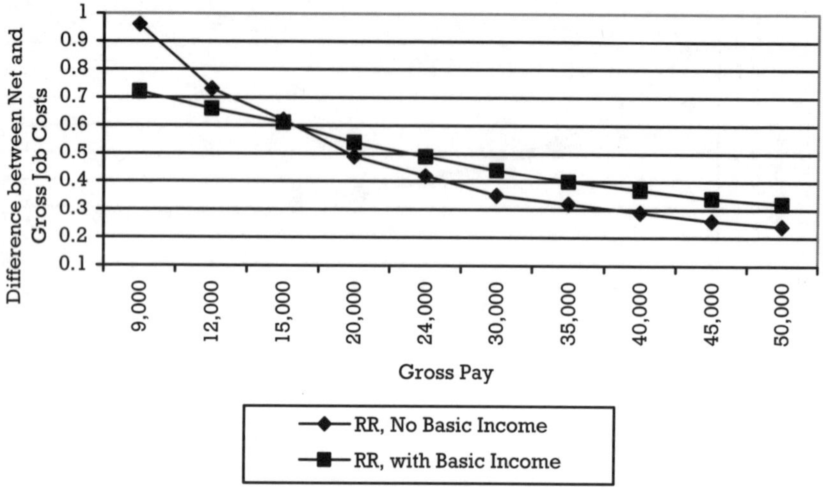
1
0.9
0.8
0.7
0.6
0.5
0.4
0.3
0.2
0.1
Difference between Net and Gross Job Costs
9,000
12,000
15,000
20,000
24,000
30,000
35,000
40,000
45,000
50,000
Gross Pay
RR, No Basic Income
RR, with Basic Income

Source: Author's calculations based on Budget 2000

Figure 5.8: Replacement Ratios, Married Couple, Two Incomes, Two Children, Current and with Basic Income

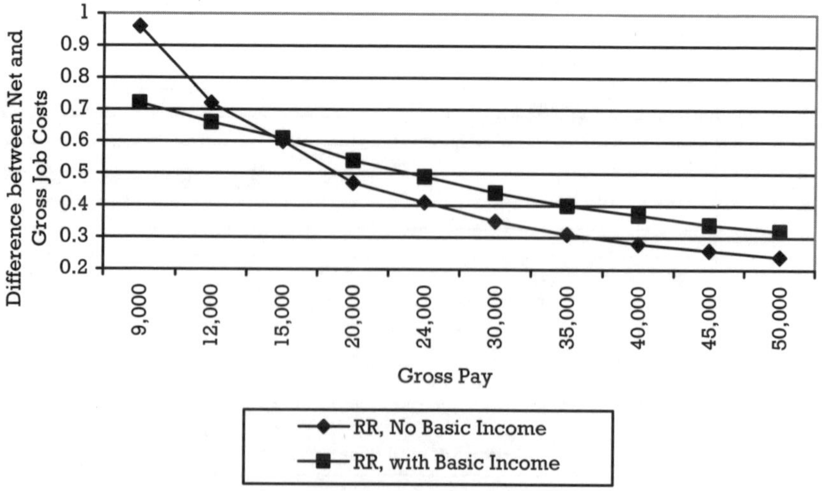
1
0.9
0.8
0.7
0.6
0.5
0.4
0.3
0.2
Difference between Net and Gross Job Costs
9,000
12,000
15,000
20,000
24,000
30,000
35,000
40,000
45,000
50,000
Gross Pay
RR, No Basic Income
RR, with Basic Income

Source: Author's calculations based on Budget 2000

The differences between the replacement ratios for unemployed workers under the current system and our Basic Income proposal show the same trends. Under a Basic Income system, the net income of the newly employed worker is higher than the net income under the current system because the worker does not lose any of their Basic Income payment when they take up a job.

Some have argued that under a Basic Income scheme, the replacement ratio for adults in "home duties" goes up, and this is possibly true, but whether it is meaningful is another question. The main reason that the replacement ratio for adults in home duties might rise under a Basic Income system is that all adults would receive the same payment, which means that workers and their spouses, whether they are in home duties, that is, working at home, or in paid employment, both receive the same payment. Both are treated equally. But under the current system, the spouse of someone on public assistance is worth only 63.2 per cent of the person on unemployment (€68.57 for spouse, €108.56 for unemployed worker); thus, the replacement ratio can be lower under the current than under a Basic Income system. The real question should be: why would anyone be interested in this statistic? What insight does it give us? Why not calculate the replacement ratio for children as well? Those in home duties have chosen to carry out these important and necessary activities, and thus have chosen not to be in the labour force as conceived by economists. Clearly, the only reason to calculate the replacement ratio of adults in home duties is to figure out what price signals would force these persons into paid employment. Here a Basic Income is clearly contrary to this view, as it gives adults in home duties the financial support to make a decision on how they will contribute to society based on what they feel is best for their families, and not forcing them into taking up a low-paying job because of economic need. This sort of analysis is either naively irrelevant or it masks a hidden agenda of undercutting all social supports for the family so as to force all adults into low-paying jobs in order

Supply of Labour

The decision to enter the labour market and seek employment is made up of many factors, some economic and some social. The most important economic factor for determining the supply of labour is economic need. Even in the most generous welfare state, only the very rich can provide a standard of living most hope for without working. This is by far the most important factor and it makes the other factors pale in comparison. The factors economists like to look at — tax and benefit levels, and wage rates — are of only marginal importance, and almost no importance when it comes to adult male workers and single female workers. As Stafford (1986) noted in his survey of 759 articles on labour supply, "labour economists have a consensus view that adult males have a labour supply which is relatively unresponsive to changes in incomes or wages while adult women have a labour supply which is quite responsive to changes in income or wage rates" (quoted in Leoni, 1994, pp. 19–20). Most people work because not working would cause serious economic hardships. Factors such as tax rates and benefit levels tend only to influence the decision to seek work if they are at levels that make increasing one's paid employment very unattractive. A few years ago, Ireland had such a situation, where certain individuals faced marginal tax and loss benefit rates of over 100 per cent. This happens when the benefit withdrawal rate, coupled with the tax on earned income, exceeds the increase in earned income. Under this type of situation, an unemployed or low-income worker would face a situation in which their gross income would go up and their net income (after taxes and benefits) would go down. Clearly, high marginal tax rates would discourage those outside of the labour force from entering the labour force and act as a poverty trap. The marginal tax rate for low income workers under a Basic Income system is the Basic Income tax rate alone (as there is no loss of benefits), and at 47.14 per cent in no way acts as a disincentive to taking up paid employment or for increasing hours worked.

LABOUR MARKET AND COMPETITIVENESS

In our discussion of competitiveness in Chapter 4, we used the *Annual Competitiveness Report 2000* of the National Competitiveness Council as our starting point for looking at how a Basic Income policy would affect the competitiveness of the Irish economy. Of the seven aspects of competitiveness mentioned in that report, we determined that three have the possibility of being influenced by a Basic Income policy: Social Partnership, People and Costs. Many of the factors that fall into the People and Costs categories relate to labour market issues. As we stated in Chapter 4, the labour market aspects of these competitiveness categories will be analysed in this chapter. Here we see that tax and social welfare policies generally will affect the labour market in two ways: the demand for labour by businesses, and the supply of labour offered to employers. The People category of competitiveness indicators highlights *work incentives* as an important factor in competitiveness. These incentives mostly relate to the willingness of workers to offer their labour to employers, although tax policy can also theoretically influence the willingness of employers to hire workers.

People

The first aspect of people considered by the NCC is education. Higher education and lifelong learning are very important for the new economy and one of the projected flexibilities that the new labour markets will need is the ability for workers to continue to improve their human capital (acquire new skills and training). Traditionally, once a student has finished their higher education, they received their diploma and were mostly done with their formal education (although it should be noted that many of the professions require continuous education of some form or another, and most non-professional occupations provide most of the necessary skills on the job site). As we saw in Chapter 4, the labour market of the new economy will require not only greater levels of education and training, but also the flexibility for workers to be able to move from work to education and back to work many times over during their working lives. A Basic Income reduces the need, in low income households, for the income provided by young adults who leave school to help support their families. A Basic Income policy supports this type of flexibility, as it allows individuals to attain higher levels of education, and to return for more training and skill attainment after their formal education is completed. This flexibility comes from the Basic Income payment, which comes without stigma[2] and which helps to support the worker who has left the paid labour force to re-enter education. Thus a Basic Income system promotes greater investment in human capital by supporting access to higher education. Furthermore, by supporting parents in home duties a Basic Income system promotes primary and secondary education, as it allows parents to take a more active role in their children's education.

We have already discussed many of the factors in the NCC report regarding work incentives. A Basic Income system reduces the tax wedge on low and moderate workers, has a minimal impact on the country's tax/GDP ratio, reduces the effective tax rate for most workers — especially low and moderate income workers — and has a marginal tax rate that does not act as a disincentive to taking up a job or increasing one's hours worked. Our Basic Income proposal will have no effect on the non-labour costs, as these remain the same. However, it is an important adjustment to the rise in the incidence of part-time employment. This rise is a reaction to the need for flexibility in the labour market and there is very little that can be done to change this trend (outside of dramatically increasing the level of regulation of the labour market). The problem, of course, with this rise in the incidence of part-time employment is that

Changing Labour Markets 101

not all of it is voluntary; many of the part-time workers need a full-time income but are only able to get part-time work. A Basic Income system helps to support these workers as it supplements their income. It also helps to support those part-time workers who want to limit their hours worked because of family responsibilities, thus allowing them to have more choice in their labour supply decisions. Our Basic Income proposal would likely lead to a reduction of hours worked in paid employment by married females, though we will also likely see in many households a redistribution of paid work and home duties for both adults living in a household, as a Basic Income system provides considerably more flexibility in making these decisions. Recent government publications have implicit arguments that it is necessary for there to be an increase in married women's paid labour market participation and the NCC report explicitly argues for such an increase. These arguments assume that the current contributions of those in home duties or caregivers is not valuable and does not make a valuable contribution to society, and that instead these people should take up a paid job so as to contribute to the market economy. This reasoning ignores the real value of household production and the social economy. Reductions in these activities will certainly lead to higher costs elsewhere in the economy and society and before Ireland goes down this road there needs to be a full and open debate on this issue.

Labour Costs

In Chapter 4, we reviewed the role of labour costs in Ireland's overall competitiveness of the Irish economy. We saw that it was one of the contributing factors in Ireland's recent economic success (though certainly not the only factor). In Table 4.2, we saw that Ireland's total hourly compensation was well below that of the US, the UK, France, Germany, The Netherlands and Japan and in Figures 4.5 and 4.6 we saw that the trend in labour costs in Ireland has been downward, while the trend for Ireland's trading partners has been rising (although both the

OECD and EU, since 1995, have had falling labour costs when compared with the US). In this section, we will look at how a Basic Income policy might affect labour costs in Ireland.

A review of the literature on Basic Income shows that there are two arguments advanced in relation to how a Basic Income system would affect labour costs. On the one hand, economists such as James Meade have argued that a Basic Income system would promote full employment because it would allow wages to fall (in effect creating wage substitution) and, according to standard economic theory, when the price of something falls (in this case the wage rate) then the demand for it will go up. Critics of Basic Income from the left frequently see this as a major drawback of a Basic Income system, while conservative supporters see it as a plus.[3] On the other hand, many promoters of a Basic Income system argue that it will support the lower end of the wage scale, thus increasing wages for those in low income, and leading to less income inequality. Clearly, both of these effects cannot happen, so a key question is: how will a Basic Income system influence wage rates and labour costs?

Wages are not simply the price of labour, and wages are not determined in the same manner as commodity prices or other prices that are determined in competitive markets. The institutional structure of any particular labour market plays a key role in determining wage levels, both absolute and relative. As Ireland now has a statutory minimum wage, a Basic Income policy cannot lead to wage substitution, at least not below the minimum wage levels. For workers with wages above the average, there is little evidence to suggest that a Basic Income policy could lead to wage substitution. These workers often have considerable bargaining power and would be able to successfully resist any such attempt. Workers with low to moderate wages typically do not have the protection of unions and other forms of institutionalised power and thus have more of a risk. Under the current climate in Ireland, with unemployment at historically low levels, there is no reason to believe that wage substitution would take place, as labour is currently scarce. If unemploy-

Changing Labour Markets 103

ment was high, this might be a concern, though again it would depend on specific characteristics of each job category and labour market. With a tight labour market, it is more likely that a Basic Income system will strengthen the lower end of the labour market rather than hurt it.

The strengthening of the lower end of the labour market is a concern among many economists and government officials in most OECD countries. The fear is that a rise in wages will lead to either falling cost competitiveness or inflation. Both fears are valid only if we look at wages outside of the context of productivity growth. However, in the context of high productivity growth (according to the NCC's report, Ireland leads all the countries considered in their report in productivity, growing at a rate of 3.75 per cent from 1994–99, compared with the EU average growth rate of 1.6 per cent), it is possible to have both rising wages and falling labour costs. Given the developments discussed in Chapter 6, especially the growth in wage inequality and the declining share of labour income as a percentage of total income, some attention should be paid towards strengthening the lower end of the wage scale. A Basic Income system directly helps these individuals in terms of income support, but will also help them by promoting greater productivity growth at the low end of the wage scale. The ultimate goal should be to increase the productivity levels of Irish workers to the levels of other OECD countries and not to be permanently in the position of competing through a low wage strategy.

Endnotes

[1] For a detailed analysis of the issue of labour market flexibility, the best starting point is Guy Standing's book *Global Labour Flexibility* (1999).

[2] The lack of any stigma of a basic income has many benefits. People on public assistance are less competitive in the job market merely because they were on public assistance. This is one of the reasons for the low take-up of FIS, for it signals the employer of an inadequacy in the employee. As everyone receives a Basic Income, there is no attached stigma.

[3] See Clark and Kavanagh (1996), "Basic Income, Inequality and Unemployment: Rethinking the Linkages between Work and Welfare", *Journal of Economic Issues*, June, Vol. 30, pp. 399–406, for a discussion on the conservative and liberal arguments for and against Basic Income.

Chapter 6

BASIC INCOME AND ECONOMIC PROGRESS FOR ALL

In the previous chapters, we have highlighted some of the remarkable economic progress the Irish economy has achieved in the past decade. In Chapter 4, we looked at the factors that promote competitiveness in the "new economy" of the 21st century, paying particular attention to the factors that have promoted Ireland's recent economic success and how Ireland can continue to improve its competitive position in the world economy. In Chapter 5, we looked at how the new economy is changing the labour market in Ireland, and elsewhere, and how the increase in labour market flexibility has the negative side-effect of decreasing economic security and promoting greater income inequality. These trends are not only likely to continue; they will get worse. Chapters 4 and 5 thus show how a Basic Income system promotes greater efficiency, especially given the requirements of technological change and globalisation. In this chapter we take an in-depth look at the trends in income inequality and poverty in Ireland and how our Basic Income proposal promotes greater equity. Taken together, these three chapters argue that, with a Basic Income system, Ireland can promote both equity and efficiency.

There should be no doubt that the economic success of Ireland's recent past has not reached all Irish citizens; a substantial portion of Irish society is being left behind. Under the current "rules of the game", the new economy generates inequality at the same time as it generates wealth and productivity gains.

This is the case for the simple reason that none of the advanced capitalist economies have adopted new institutions and policies to ensure that the benefits of the new economy are shared by all. Given that so much of the new economy, especially the development of the technology and creation of the necessary infrastructure, is in fact the direct result of government programmes and taxpayer subsidies, it is a matter of simple justice that society as a whole share in the benefits. Furthermore, the new economy is also called the "knowledge economy", the culmination of all the ideas and insights of the human race.

The fact that a small percentage of the population can monopolise the lion's share of the benefit of that knowledge, and that many would be left out completely, is nothing short of a crime, both within Ireland and the world as a whole. The current system of distributing income is based on each individual's ownership of saleable market goods and services and other claims on social output, such as pensions or social welfare payments. These claims are derived from the political history of each society and are based on the power of specific groups to demand and receive a share of the social product. But the majority of the benefits of production go to those with some control over the required inputs needed to produce the national output. Workers control their labour and if their skills are in short supply or particularly valuable, they will receive a high income. Owners of raw materials, the means of production (factories, etc.), money to lend and property to rent, also receive a share based on their relative bargaining positions and importance in the production process.

In the new economy, the great addition to the production process is knowledge. To receive a large share of the benefits of this addition to output, one must control and monopolise this knowledge. This is where the wealth of the new economy comes from. While one can argue that there are benefits to society in this knowledge being privately controlled and used — i.e. that there are efficiency benefits due to this arrangement — one can also claim that no such argument exists for all the "economic rents" (income beyond competitive rates) created by this "knowledge-based economy" should remain in these same hands. Such high returns in this "winner-take-all" economy are not necessary in order to provide incentives for these entrepreneurs; they will work just as hard for much smaller returns than they are currently getting. Until a new system is designed to ensure that all benefit from the new economy, persistent poverty and growing income inequality will remain a key feature.

This rise in inequality and poverty is seen very clearly in the countries that have made the greatest institutional adaptations to the new economy, and is most evident in the countries that have been able to accomplish significant job growth in the past decade (with Ireland and the United States being the prime examples). In this chapter, we will first look at the recent trends in poverty and income inequality in Ireland. Here we see that the normal tendency of "a rising tide lifting all boats" no longer holds to the extent that it did in the "old economy". In the second part of this chapter, we will examine how a Basic Income policy in general, and our proposal in particular, will impact on the poverty levels and the distribution of income in Ireland.

POVERTY AND INCOME INEQUALITY IN IRELAND

Ireland has a long tradition of high rates of poverty and income inequality, stemming from its historical experience as an English colony. This historical context is important to note, as the historical experience of a country is one of the most powerful factors in explaining international differences in the levels of income inequality and poverty. A look at the rankings of countries based on their levels of inequality show the five major English-speaking countries (four being former English colonies, the other being England) as concentrated at the top of the inequality list. In fact, they include the top four most unequal distributions of income, with Canada breaking the trend by coming in seventh. This is especially true for final income (post-tax and transfer) but it is also true for market income rankings, although here they have more company. This is demonstrated in Table 6.1, showing the rankings in the late 1980s, taken from the OECD study on income inequality and from other sources. Some analysts suggest that this phenomenon stems from the English system of common law and the primacy of the rights of property, and no doubt this is part of the answer (as is the creation of great inequality during the colonial period, i.e. the stealing of land and property from the indigenous people and the concentration of these in the hands of those allied to the colonial power, and the legacy of inequality and poverty that this past generates).

Table 6.1: Inequality Ranks, OECD Countries, Late 1980s

Country	Year	Gini	Atkinson 0.5	Atkinson 1.0	Ave. Rank
US	1986	34.1 (1)	10.0 (1)	26.3 (2)	1.33
Ireland	**1987**	**33.0 (2)**	**9.4 (2)**	**24.4 (4)**	**2.67**
UK	1986	30.4 (5)	8.4 (3)	26.4 (1)	3.00
Australia	1989	31.0 (3)	8.3 (4)	19.9 (7)	4.67
France	1984	29.6 (6)	7.8 (6)	21.9 (5)	5.67
Italy	1986	31.0 (4)	8.0 (5)	15.6 (9)	6.00
Netherlands	1987	26.8 (8)	6.4 (8)	26.2 (3)	6.33
Canada	1987	28.9 (7)	7.0 (7)	16.8 (8)	7.33
Denmark	1987	25.7 (9)	6.2 (9)	21.1 (6)	8.00
Germany	1984	25.0 (10)	5.2 (10)	10.1 (13)	11.00
Belgium	1988	23.5 (11)	5.0 (11)	13.4 (11)	11.00
Sweden	1987	22.0 (13)	4.7 (12)	14.1 (10)	11.67
Norway	1986	23.4 (12)	4.7 (12)	10.9 (12)	12.00

Source: Luxembourg Income Study Inequality Indices, http://lissy.ceps.lu/ineq.htm

As we can see from Table 6.1, the inequality ranking is slightly sensitive to how inequality is measured. For this reason, we have given three different measures and the average ranking for each country. Later in this chapter, we provide other measures of changes in inequality in Ireland. In Table 6.2, we give one measure of income inequality for the same countries given above, for the mid-1990s.

Table 6.2: Inequality Ranks, OECD Countries, Mid-1990s

Country	Year	Gini
US	1997	37.2
Ireland	**1994/5**	**36.0***
UK	1995	34.4
Italy	1995	34.2
Australia	1994	31.2
France	1994	28.8
Canada	1994	28.5
Netherlands	1994	25.3
Germany	1994	26.1
Belgium	1996	26.0
Norway	1995	23.8
Denmark	1992	23.6
Sweden	1995	22.1

Source: Luxembourg Income Study Inequality Indices, http://lissy.ceps.lu/ineq.htm.
* From Collins and Kavanagh, 1998.

An examination of the trends in pre-tax and transfer (i.e. market-determined) and post-tax and transfer (i.e. after government intervention) poverty rates in the advanced capitalist economies reveals that the trend of the 1990s is towards increasing market-generated levels of income inequality and, along with this, levels of poverty. In Figure 6.1 below, we see that in just about all of the countries presented below there has been an increase in pre-tax and transfer levels of poverty. This indicates that the market forces of the new economy are generating higher levels of poverty. Only The Netherlands and Sweden are contrary to this trend.

110   *The Basic Income Guarantee*

Figure 6.1: Pre- and Post-Tax Transfer Poverty Rates

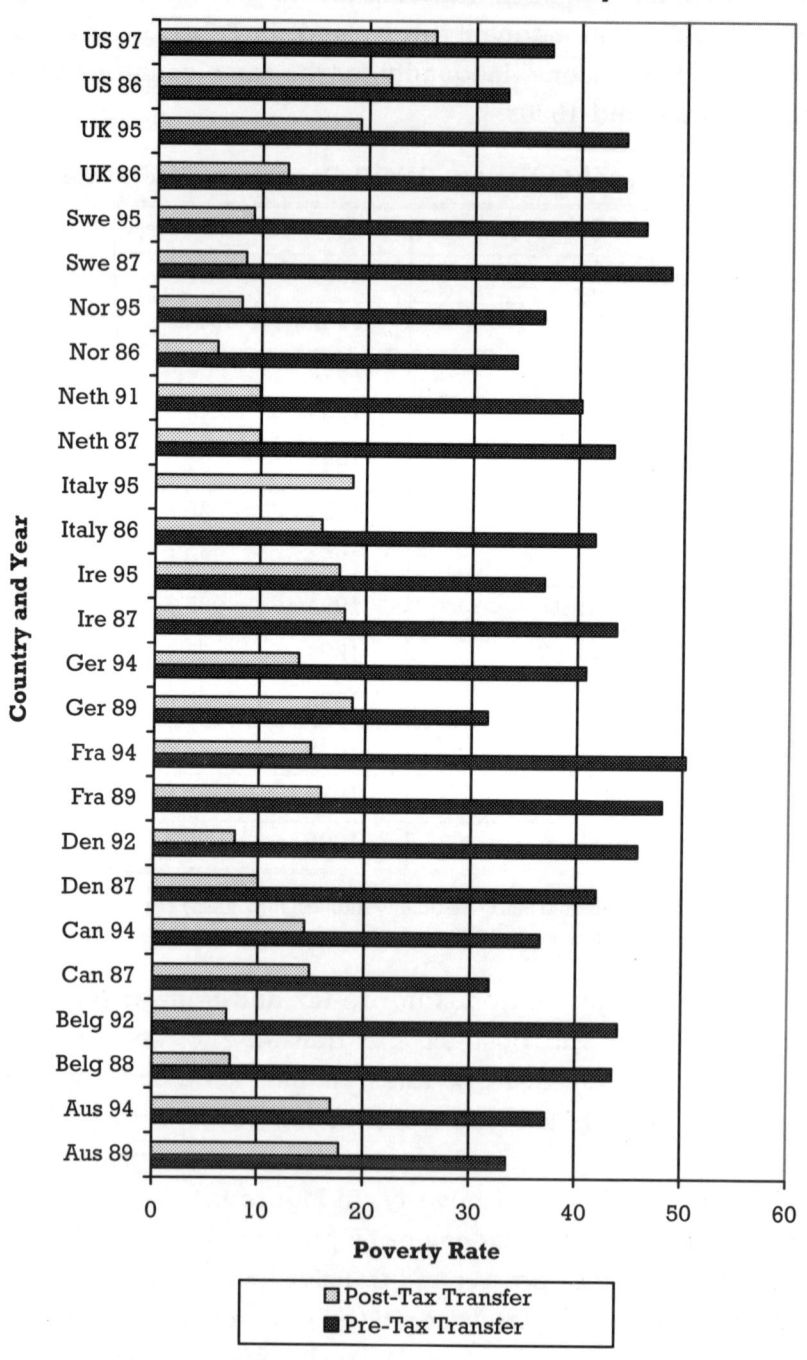

□ Post-Tax Transfer
■ Pre-Tax Transfer

Source: LIS and author (Ireland, 1995)

If we compare the data contained above with that in the previous chapter on competitiveness, we see that the countries that have achieved significant growth in employment (or reduced unemployment) have also tended to have corresponding increases in income inequality and poverty levels. Moreover, the countries that have kept poverty levels from increasing have generally had stagnant economies, slow economic growth and little improvement in the levels of unemployment, with The Netherlands being the most notable exception to this rule. It seems, as stated in the introduction of this book, that countries are faced with the choice of either economic growth that mostly benefits the already well off or no economic growth at all. These facts are indicative of the dynamics of the new economy and the costs of fighting poverty and income inequality using the methods of the "old economy".

THE CASE OF IRELAND

Looking at the evidence from Ireland's recent past, we see that there was some progress towards lowering poverty and income inequality in the 1970s and the mid-1980s; however, this trend was reversed in the late 1980s and 1990s. Looking first at poverty levels, we see in Table 6.2 that poverty rates, particularly for the poorest, have risen sharply in the mid-1990s.

Table 6.2: Percentage of Population in Households in Poverty, 1973–97

Extent of Relative Poverty	1973	1980	1987	1994	1997
Below 40% line	8	8	7	7	10
Below 50% line	15	16	19	21	22
Below 60% line	25	27	30	34	35

Source: National Economic and Social Council (1999), *Opportunities, Challenges and Capacities for Choice*, p. 17.

The National Anti-Poverty Strategy (1997) stated that high unemployment, especially long-term unemployment, was a prime cause of the persistence of poverty in Ireland; yet this rise took place while unemployment rates were falling.

The recent issue of *Monitoring Poverty Trends* (ESRI, 2001) shows how the new economy is failing many low income households in Ireland. This can be seen by looking at the percentage of households falling below the 50 per cent relative income poverty line and the risk for households of falling below the 50 per cent relative poverty line. These are provided in Tables 6.3 and 6.4 respectively. In Table 6.3, we see some of the changes in the composition of households under the 50 per cent relative income poverty line. From 1994 to 1997, households headed by unemployed and farmers fell significantly, while all other groups rose, with significant increases for employees and retirees. Some of these trends seem to be reversed in 1998, especially for households headed by employees and self-employed.

Table 6.3: Breakdown of Households Below 50 per cent Relative Income Poverty Line by Labour Force Status of Head, Living in Ireland Surveys 1994 and 1997

Labour Force Status	1994	1997	1998
Employee	5.3	7.3	4.0
Self-employed	6.6	6.2	5.2
Farmer	8.0	5.0	6.2
Unemployed	30.3	18.9	15.4
Ill/disabled	9.6	9.1	8.8
Retired	10.1	17.9	21.2
Home Duties	30.2	35.7	39.2
All	100	100	100

Source: ESRI (2001), *Monitoring Poverty Trends*, p. 24.

Table 6.4 shows the risk for households of falling below the 50 per cent line, by labour market status of the head of household. Here we see increases for employees, self-employed, retired and home duties for 1994 to 1997, with reductions for employees and self-employed in 1998. Furthermore, those out of the labour market (ill/disabled, retired and home duties) have also had significant increases in their risk of falling below the poverty line.

Table 6.4: Risk of Falling Below 50 per cent Relative Income Poverty Line by Labour Force Status of Household Head, Living in Ireland Surveys, 1994, 1997 and 1998

Labour Force Status	1994	1997	1998
Employee	2.8	4.0	2.3
Self-employed	15.1	17.1	15.8
Farmer	21.5	16.3	22.0
Unemployed	57.3	54.9	56.2
Ill/disabled	50.0	60.4	72.6
Retired	10.2	23.3	28.7
Home Duties	33.2	48.6	58.4
All	18.6	22.3	24.3

Source: ESRI (2001), *Monitoring Poverty Trends*, p. 24.

Furthermore, as the Inter-Departmental Group report on the impact of the minimum wage (ESRI, 1999) concluded, the introduction of a minimum wage in Ireland will have little effect in lowering poverty levels. New approaches for helping those at the bottom half of the economic ladder must be found if all are to participate and share in the benefits of the new economy.

CHANGES IN INCOME DISTRIBUTION

In Tables 6.5, 6.6 and 6.7, we present data on the changes in the distribution of income in Ireland from the 1970s to the mid-1990s. In Table 6.5, we show the aggregate share of direct income (income from work or property) by household deciles. In Table 6.6, we see the shares of aggregate disposable household income by decile, which includes the effects of tax and transfer on household incomes. In Table 6.7, we provide three measures of income inequality for both direct and disposable household incomes for the time period under consideration.

Table 6.5: Distribution of Direct Income, 1973–2000 (%)

Decile	1973	1980	1987	1994/95	1999/2000
Bottom	0.01	0.00	0.38	0.29	0.26
2nd	1.18	0.54	1.00	0.92	0.81
3rd	3.78	2.84	1.39	1.27	2.07
4th	6.06	5.70	3.26	3.10	4.22
5th	7.65	7.68	6.05	5.92	6.60
6th	9.25	9.46	8.73	8.80	9.07
7th	11.27	11.49	11.55	11.76	11.52
8th	13.82	14.24	15.09	15.43	14.61
9th	17.73	18.34	20.08	19.90	19.02
Top	29.24	29.72	32.46	32.61	31.84

Source: Collins and Kavanagh (1998), *Household Budget Survey*, various issues. May not equal 100 per cent due to rounding.

Table 6.6: Distribution of Disposable Income, 1973–2000 (%)

Decile	1973	1980	1987	1994/95	1999/2000
Bottom	2.67	3.15	2.28	2.23	1.93
2nd	3.03	3.20	3.74	3.49	3.16
3rd	5.11	4.62	5.11	4.75	4.52
4th	6.56	6.38	6.41	6.16	6.01
5th	7.79	7.68	7.71	7.63	7.67
6th	9.07	9.03	9.24	9.37	9.35
7th	10.83	13.17	11.16	11.41	11.20
8th	12.86	12.64	13.39	13.64	13.48
9th	16.06	15.55	16.48	16.67	16.78
Top	26.03	24.58	24.48	24.67	25.90

Source: Collins and Kavanagh (1998), *Household Budget Survey*, various issues. May not equal 100 per cent due to rounding.

Table 6.7: Changes in the Measures of Inequality of Direct and Disposable Income, 1973–94/95

Year	Gini Coefficient	Coefficient of Variation	Theil Index
1973 Direct	0.45	0.83	0.35
1980 Direct	0.47	0.86	0.39
1987 Direct	0.52	0.97	0.46
1994/95 Direct	0.52	0.98	0.47
1973 Disposable	0.35	0.67	0.20
1980 Disposable	0.34	0.63	0.19
1987 Disposable	0.35	0.64	0.19
1994/95 Disposable	0.36	0.65	0.20

Source: Collins and Kavanagh (1998), *Household Budget Survey*, various issues.

From Table 6.7, we get the broadest perspective of changes in income inequality in Ireland from the 1970s to the 1990s. The general trend is a slight decrease in inequality from the 1970s to the mid-1980s, with a reversal from the mid 1980s to the mid-1990s. Tables 6.5 and 6.6 include information from the 1999/2000 Household Budget Survey, which was released in late 2001. It shows that both the direct and disposable incomes for those at the lowest income deciles have lost some of their share in aggregate income, with the bottom four deciles losing share of aggregate disposable income. And even though the direct income share of the wealthiest 20 per cent of households experienced a decrease in their share of direct income, their share of disposable income went up, and for the top decile it rose 1.23 percentage points, the biggest change of all income deciles. What this means is that government policy (changes in taxes and benefits) produced an increase in the share of disposable income to the top decile even though their share in aggregate income due to market forces (direct income) had fallen. This bias in government policy towards tax cuts, which typically benefit the well-off, and against the social welfare system, has recently been demonstrated in the ESRI's Budget Perspectives (2001, p. 48) where it is noted that "the total welfare system, including child benefit, received under 10 per cent of the total resources over and above indexation, while the tax system was allocated about 90 per cent". It is no wonder that after-tax inequality rose between 1994/95 and 1999/2000.

Sources of Income Inequality

One of the reasons for increased income inequality in Ireland, as in many other developed countries, is the fall in labour income as a percentage of national income and the rise in property income. We see in Figure 6.2 that profit income has been rising and that wage income has been falling.

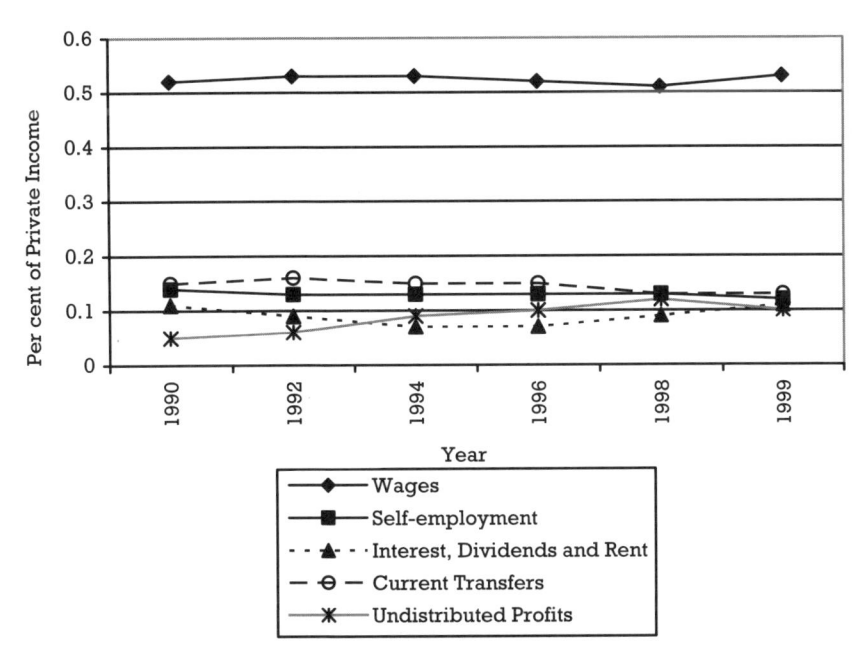

Figure 6.2: Capital Income Share of Business Income, Ireland and EU

[Chart showing Per cent of Private Income from 1990 to 1999 with series: Wages, Self-employment, Interest, Dividends and Rent, Current Transfers, Undistributed Profits]

Source: CSO, National Income and Expenditure Accounts

The rise of property income (profits and rents) goes disproportionately to the already affluent, whereas the fall in the share in wages and self-employment income hits the middle-income households particularly hard. The dramatic rise in income going to capital in the business sector is also seen quite clearly in Figure 6.3, where we see Ireland's share compared with the EU average. Ireland is now at the EU average.

While wages have fallen as a percentage of total income, the distribution of wages, wage inequality, seems to have been increasing in Ireland. Although the data here is less complete than we would like, it does show a dramatic increase in wage inequality, especially in the late 1980s up to 1995 (the last year for which data is available). This is seen in the Wage Theil Index, calculated by James Kenneth Galbraith and the University of Texas Inequality Project, given below in Figure 6.4.

Figure 6.3: Capital Income Share of Business Income, Ireland and the EU

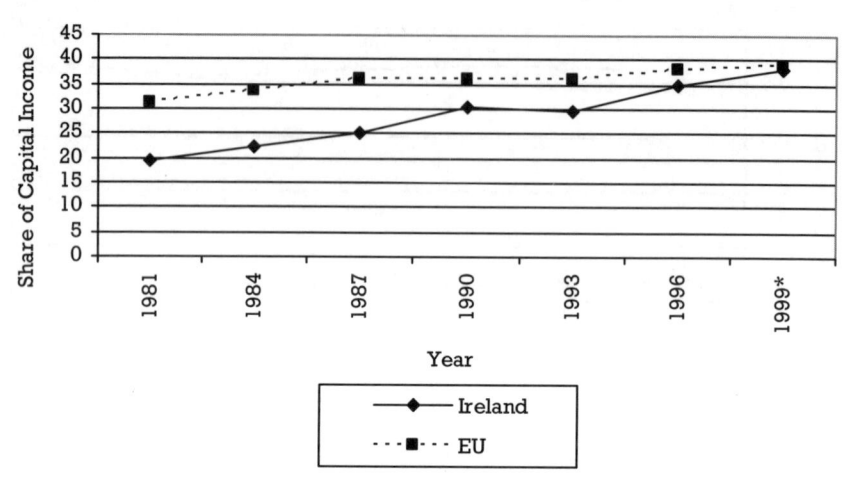

* Projection
Source: *OECD Economic Outlook,* 1998

Figure 6.4: Wage Inequality in Ireland, 1963–97

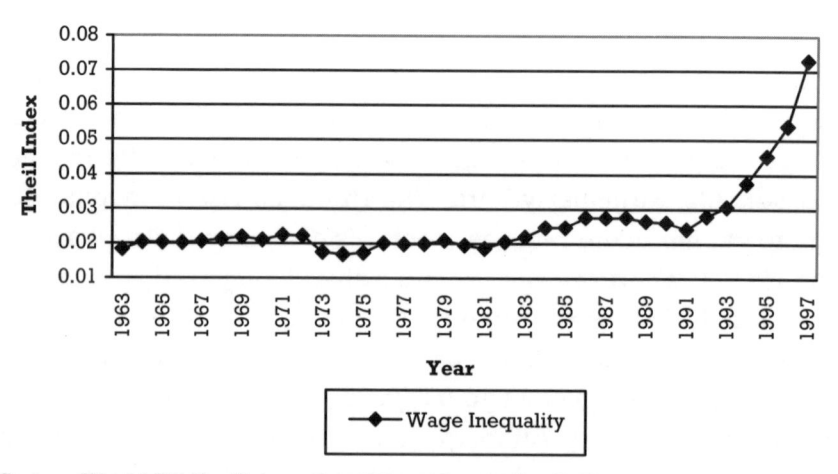

Source: World Theils, University of Texas Inequality Project

The rise in wage inequality has been shown in other measures of wage inequality. In Table 6.8, we see the trends in earnings distribution in Ireland and other OECD countries from 1987 to 1994. Ireland had the largest increase in this period.

Table 6.8: Trends in Earnings Distribution, Ireland and Selected Countries, 1987–94 (ratio of top decile to bottom decile, gross earnings)

Country	1987	1994	Change
Canada	4.44	4.20	-0.24
Germany	2.54	2.32	-0.22
Belgium	2.44	2.24	-0.20
Finland	2.52	2.38	-0.14
Japan	3.15	3.02	-0.13
Sweden	2.09	2.13	0.04
Australia	2.81	2.87	0.06
Netherlands	2.53	2.59	0.06
France	3.19	3.28	0.09
United Kingdom	3.20	3.31	0.11
New Zealand	2.92	3.05	0.13
Austria	3.47	3.66	0.19
Italy	2.42	2.80	0.38
Ireland	3.67	4.06	0.39

Source: Barrett et al. (1999), Table 3, cited in Kennelly and Collins (1999), p. 36.

Although it might be possible that the various national wage agreements enacted since 1996 (the last year for which data for the above measure of wage inequality is available), might have slowed this trend down or reversed it, this is not likely. These agreements have included wage moderation, which increases the decline in wage income as a share of national income and increase the share going to capital. Furthermore, high income workers are less likely to be covered by these agreements, thus there is less wage moderation for well-off workers. This, coupled with labour shortages of highly skilled workers, promotes greater wage inequality.

The obvious question for the reader to ask is: why does inequality matter? While many economists feel that growing income inequality is a sign of a healthy economy (we return to this argument below) it is worth pointing out that inequality imposes costs onto society. First, it limits the social and economic participation of those at the lower end of the economic ladder. These individuals and households have less time and means to participate in the social, economic and cultural life of the community. In the process, the whole community is made worse off. Second, income inequality is associated with many health problems and with lower life expectancy. Third, economies with higher levels of income inequality tend to be less stable than economies with lower levels of income inequality for the simple reason that more of the society's money is circulating in the purchase of goods and services and not accumulated in savings (which is income that is not spent) or on expensive imports (income that flows overseas). It is an important conclusion of John Maynard Keynes' *General Theory* that income inequality promotes unemployment (1936, Chapter 24). Lastly, income inequality is an important indicator for a country's quality of life, with higher levels of equality being associated with higher levels of happiness (assuming the aggregate level of income is the same).

Is the Rise in Income Inequality Necessary for the Prosperity of the Irish Economy?

The response of many economists and public officials to the above evidence on rising income inequality, and persistent poverty, is that it is a necessary, however regrettable, price for economic prosperity, at least in the short run. This opinion is based on the commonly held view by many economists that there is an efficiency/equality trade-off and that if you want more efficiency (economic growth) you need to sacrifice some equality. This is the view that has dominated public policy in England, Canada, New Zealand and the United States during the 1980s and has carried over to the 1990s. In an effort to promote economic efficiency, all of these countries embarked on policies that implicitly or explicitly were designed to increase the levels of income inequality, typically in the forms of tax cuts geared towards the affluent and cuts in assistance (either in terms of social welfare benefits or in regulatory and institutional supports) for workers and the poor. Whether the Reagan/ Thatcher experiment was a success in generating economic growth and progress or not is an open question (growth rates in the 1960s, when inequality was decreasing in most OECD countries, were much higher than in the 1980s and 1990s). However, it clearly was very successful in increasing income inequality.

The Reagan/Thatcher policy is not one that has had much support in Ireland, where the government has been committed to increasing social welfare benefit levels and coverage while these other countries have been slashing or eliminating them. The fact that Ireland has experienced both increasing benefit levels and rapid employment growth is evidence that a country does not have to follow the "war on the poor", as it has been called in the United States (and the fact that many of these countries did not have rapid employment growth is further evidence of the lack of success of this experiment).

POVERTY IMPACTS OF BASIC INCOME PROPOSAL

In this section we will look at how our Basic Income proposal will impact the poverty levels in Ireland, comparing it with a continuation of the status quo. We will do this by simulating poverty level changes using our 1994/95 HBS model. We will also compare our results with some of the forecasts of the ESRI's micro-simulation model from their *Monitoring Poverty Trends* (ESRI, 1999) study. Table 6.9 presents the percentage of persons below the relative income poverty lines for 1994, 1997 and projected to 2001.

Table 6.9: Percentage of Persons below Relative Poverty Lines, 1994, 1997, and 2001

% of Persons Below	1994 (SWITCH)	1994/5 HBS	1998 (LIS)	2001 (SWITCH)	2001 BI No SSF HBS Model	2001 BI With SSF HBS Model
40% of average	5.4	5.8	9.4	11.5	0.16	0.0
50% of average	18.9	17.5	19.4	21.6	6.08	0.0
60% of average	30.1	31.9	28.8	31.8	19.57	19.57

Source: Monitoring Poverty Trends (ESRI, 2001); and author's calculations.

SWITCH = ESRI simulated rates; LIS = actual results from ESRI's *Living in Ireland* survey for 1998; HBS = actual results of 1994/95 Household Budget Survey Anonymised Microdata Files; HBS Model = Author's simulations based on a model derived from the 1994/95 HBS; SSF = Social Solidarity Fund.

In Table 6.9, we see both simulated and actual estimates of the percentage of persons below various relative poverty lines. The estimates for 1994–2001 all show the same basic trend of rising poverty rates, especially amongst the lower cut-off levels (40 per cent and 50 per cent). From the above table, we see that our Basic Income proposal as it is currently formulated is an effective policy for reducing poverty levels. In Table 6.10, we see the impact on child poverty in Ireland of our Basic Income proposal.

Table 6.10: Child Poverty in Ireland, 1995 and 2001 with BI

% of Children below	1995 HBS	2001 BI with SSF HBS Model
40%	7.3	0.0
50%	23.2	0.0
60%	36.6	22.18

Our Basic Income proposal, with the Social Solidarity Fund, effectively eliminates material poverty, raising all households to at least 50 per cent of the median household income. This is no small achievement.

INCOME DISTRIBUTION EFFECTS

In this section, we look at how our Basic Income proposal will affect the distribution of income in Ireland. In Table 6.11, we see the average household weekly disposable income by income decile. This table shows us how the benefits of our Basic Income proposal are being distributed. First it shows how each decile's average disposable income has increased from 1994/95 to 1999/2000. It then gives each decile's average disposable income under our proposed Basic Income system. Finally, it gives the changes, in units and in percentages, from moving from 1999/2000 to our Basic Income proposal.

Table 6.11: Average Household Weekly Disposable Income by Decile, 1994/95, 1999/2000 and 2001 with BI (current punts)

Decile	1994/95	1999/2000	2001 BI	Change 99/00 to 2001 BI	% Change 99/00 to 2001 BI
Bottom	69.30	83.67	119.45	35.78	42.76
2nd	105.47	137.37	198.46	61.09	44.47
3rd	139.49	196.44	266.63	70.19	35.73
4th	174.59	261.24	337.98	76.74	29.38
5th	220.11	333.14	413.20	80.06	24.03
6th	268.85	406.17	483.31	77.14	18.99
7th	334.44	486.45	548.35	61.90	12.72
8th	408.47	585.51	633.75	48.24	8.24
9th	494.60	728.91	745.39	16.48	2.26
Top	688.53	1125.22	1150.64	25.42	2.26

Table 6.11 demonstrates one of the central points made in *Pathways to a Basic Income* (Clark and Healy, 1997) — that if a Basic Income system is phased in over a few years (during a period of income growth), it can be done without creating any income losers. Here we see that our proposal is very progressive in that the percentage increases of those in the bottom five deciles are higher than those of the upper five deciles. In fact,

with the exception of the second decile being higher than the first, it is perfectly progressive.

BASIC INCOME COMPARED WITH CURRENT DISTRIBUTION WITHOUT BASIC INCOME

In Table 6.12 below we see a comparison of the estimated average household weekly income by decile for 2001 with a Basic Income and 2001 without a Basic Income. Here we see that the income of the top four deciles without the Basic Income system is higher (although the change in the seventh decile is marginal) than with the Basic Income system. This table indicates that a Basic Income system is an effective way in spreading the benefits of economic progress, for without such a system the benefits end up going mostly to the affluent.

Table 6.12: Mean Household Weekly Income by Decile, 2001 with Basic Income and 2001 without Basic Income (current punts)

Decile	2001 BI	2001 no BI	Difference
Bottom	119.45	90.98	28.47
2nd	198.46	150.05	48.41
3rd	266.63	216.29	50.34
4th	337.98	291.52	46.46
5th	413.20	373.88	39.32
6th	483.31	458.26	25.05
7th	548.35	550.72	−2.37
8th	633.75	663.89	−30.14
9th	745.39	827.14	−81.75
Top	1150.64	1278.42	−127.78

As we saw in the first chapter of this study, reducing poverty and income inequality is a primary stated goal for the National Economic and Social Council, and most other public policy groups in Ireland. Under the rules of the "old economy", the elimination of poverty and income inequality was achieved by active intervention in how incomes are determined, in the various factor markets for wages, rents, interest and profits. This was accomplished most successfully by the Scandinavian countries, and their low levels of inequality and poverty attest to the success of these efforts. Furthermore, these economies outperformed the OECD in many key economic categories during the 1960 and 1970s. However, as we have seen earlier in this book, the old rules started to become obsolete during the 1980s, and these countries have not had much success in competing in the new economy. It should be obvious to all that Ireland is not going to be able to duplicate the welfare states of Sweden, Norway and Denmark and continue to compete successfully in the new economy. A Basic Income system allows Ireland to pursue both greater efficiency and greater equity.

Chapter 7

SOME ALTERNATIVES TO OUR BASIC INCOME PROPOSAL

There are almost an infinite number of variations on the Basic Income theme and our Basic Income proposal is merely an example of what such a system could look like in Ireland. Although it is loosely based on some actual Basic Income proposals, it is certainly open to changes and alternations. In this chapter we will briefly look at some possible alternatives to our Basic Income proposal. As we have stated throughout this study, any actual Basic Income system will be the result of the political process.

A Basic Income system is one in which a universal income is paid to all citizens on a universal basis. A participatory Basic Income does not have the characteristic of universality and maintains some system of means testing. Thus one variation on a Basic Income system is to drop the universality facet and limit the eligibility to some form of social or economic participation. Such participation criteria could be broad so as to include all forms of social participation, including home care and volunteer work, or it could be narrow and only include those participating in the market aspects of society (working or looking for work). As such a change brings back many of the poverty and unemployment traps we are seeking to eliminate, as well as other undesirable elements of the present system (such as the stigmas that would arise in the political process of deciding which forms of participation are valid and which are not), we will not be developing such an option here. The other two primary features of a Basic Income system that are subject to variations are the level of payments and the mode of financing. Changes in the payment level will have more or less of the income distribution and poverty impacts already displayed in previous chapters, in the same direction as the change in payment levels. Reductions in the payment level would require keeping some form of the current social welfare system and thus complicate the analysis considerably, and it also defeats the purpose of a Basic Income system. In this chapter, we will look at some alternative methods of financing a Basic Income in Ireland.

FUNDING/TAXATION OPTIONS

In looking at alternative methods of funding a Basic Income system, it is important to keep in mind the overall theme of this study: a 21st century economy needs a 21st century system of distributing the benefits of economic progress. It is reasonable to start by asking the broader question of how tax revenues should be collected in this new institutional framework. The scope of such a question is very broad indeed and no doubt numerous books and articles can, and hopefully will, be written on this subject. We will only touch upon some of the issues as they pertain to Basic Income.

When examining any questions regarding the methods by which governments collect revenues, economists often start with Adam Smith's four maxims of taxation. In *The Wealth of Nations* (1776), Smith notes that a good tax has the following attributes: 1) all subjects contribute "as nearly as possible, in proportion to their respective abilities" (equity); 2) "[t]he time of payment, the manner of payment, the quantity to be paid, ought all to be clear and plain to the contributor, and to every other person ought to be certain, and not arbitrary" (transparency); 3) is levied "in a manner in which it is most likely to be convenient for the contributor to pay" and 4) "every tax ought to be so contrived as both to take out and to keep out of the pockets of the people as little as possible, over and above what it brings into the public treasury of the state", that is, be efficient in collection (low costs of collecting taxes) (Smith, 1976, pp. 825–26). To this list economists have, following the work of A.C. Pigou, added the attribute of correcting for externalities (and other market failures). Externalities exist when market transactions create costs or benefits that are not included in the cost or benefit calculations of either the buyer or the seller. In effect, externalities recognise that actual market prices do not fully reflect the total social costs and benefits of an economic activity or transaction, and thus generate inefficient outcomes. Taxes (and subsidies) can be used by the government to bring the prices of goods and services more in line with their true social costs and benefits.

The new economy presents many challenges to the field of public finance. As argued earlier in this book, the new economy has two outstanding characteristics: globalisation and technological change. Both changes are significant in terms of how the government can generate the necessary revenues in order to carry out its obligations. Globalisation has considerably increased the mobility of capital, giving it greater power to avoid having to pay taxes. The net effect of this improved bargaining position is that it allows capital to move to areas and countries that will tax it the least (in fact this has been a source of competitive advantage for Ireland in the past decade). Often just the existence of productive capacity in multiple countries gives a company significant power in reducing its exposure to taxation, playing each country against the others. Thus we have seen across the OECD countries a shifting of taxes away from capital and businesses and towards less mobile factors of production, such as labour.

The second factor in the new economy also presents a serious problem for raising tax revenue. Technological change has the potential to create large-scale technological unemployment and thus reduce the need for workers. This will at the same time reduce the number of taxpayers. In any case, with capital able to avoid being taxed, workers will have to pay a large share of the cost of government services out of a smaller share of aggregate income (as was demonstrated in Chapter 6). This presents a serious long-run problem for government finances over the next few decades. Additionally, the new economy is creating new forms of social costs and benefits, thus creating new externalities that need to be addressed (the Tobin tax below addresses one such externality). Furthermore, the new economy is creating new forms of wealth and incomes, many of which fall outside of the purview of most countries' systems of taxation. Thus, although this study has stayed within the realm of existing systems of revenue collection, certainly new sources will need to be developed.

Environment Tax

There is no doubt that environmentally based taxes will play a greater role in the economy of the 21st century economy, regardless of the developments of the new economy. Global warming is the quintessential externality and is the result of the social costs of production and consumption being much higher than the direct costs of production (that is, the costs that under the current system of property rights must be paid). Many economic activities contribute to this problem and their contributions (costs created) to global warming are not included in the prices paid by the producers for intermediate production or by consumers for final goods and services. This is inefficient. Any system of market exchange is based on the idea that prices reflect total costs and benefits; thus, taxes and subsidies will need to be assessed in order for there to be "correct" prices. All this is necessary and will need to happen regardless of the issues and problems that a Basic Income addresses. However, environmental taxes could play a role in the Basic Income discussion for the simple fact that environmental taxes have what is being called a "double dividend". Not only do environmental taxes correct for some serious market failures in the creation of market prices, and thus allow for more efficient market signals and behaviour, they also collect revenues for the state, revenues that could be used to help fund a Basic Income system or some other socially beneficial programme. In fact, the existence of gross inequities in the distribution of incomes and wealth is often the result of market failures (monopoly power, ignorance, luck, past distribution) and not the result of the need for market signals to clear factor markets. Thus the Basic Income payment would correct for one market failure while part of its funding mechanism, a pollution tax of some sort, would correct for another market failure.

The reduction in income tax rates due to the implementation of an environmental tax will induce employment gains. This is particularly true if the cuts are in employer social security tax contributions, more so than when they are in income tax reductions. The reasoning here is that a cut in income taxation will rarely lead to an increase in hours worked or labour supply, but that a cut in employer contributions cuts the cost of labour. If there is a possibility for substitution, then this could lead to an increase in the demand for labour.

The adoption of such a system of taxation to fund, at least partially, a Basic Income system would contribute to its efficiency effects, leading to a greater meeting of the needs of all in the population and creating more "beneficial" economic progress and less "damaging" economic progress (that is, increases in economic transactions due to environmental or social decay).

PROPERTY AND WEALTH TAX

One of the most troubling aspects of the new economy has been the fact that the new wealth created is highly concentrated. This is a separate issue from the growing inequalities in incomes, which is also a troubling creation of the new economy. In fact, the widening gap in terms of wealth ownership is far greater than that in incomes. In many ways, wealth is a better measure of "respective abilities" to pay the taxes Adam Smith mentions in his maxims of taxation. It is also a better indicator of economic security and of the property protected by the state (which Adam Smith noted is the reason governments exist in the first place, to protect the property of the affluent from the masses). Thus, a system of wealth or property taxation will correct for the negative externality of gross inequalities in ownership of wealth and property created by historical factors and economic and political power (and not as the result of contributions to output and economic and social well-being).

A tax on wealth and property is often hard to avoid, especially if the property is in the form of real estate. An additional benefit of a property tax is that it would fall disproportionately on land speculators, making the ownership of land a less attractive economic investment compared with more productive investments. This will help to stabilise property markets and cut into the "windfall profits" that have been going to property owners in Ireland, especially in the past five years.

Currently, 11 developed countries have some sort of wealth tax. Following Edward Wolff's (Wolff, 1996) work, a wealth tax for Ireland could be developed that would:

- Annually tax net worth, excluding pension wealth and household effects (and automobiles worth up to a set amount).

- The first, say, £100,000 of net worth could be exempt, eliminating most households from having to pay any wealth tax.

- The wealth tax would be filed together with the income tax.

Ireland could reintroduce a system of property tax, which it had in the mid-1990s; however, given that the new economy creates wealth that typically is not in the form of land and real estate, it would be more equitable to have some form of wealth tax that captures this new wealth. Like environmental taxes, wealth taxes have the "double dividend" effect in that they can be designed to reduce speculation in financial markets, which generates considerable inefficiencies in the "real economy" while at the same time contributing to a Basic Income system that helps to promote greater equity.

TOBIN TAX

A Tobin Tax is a sales tax on currency trades across borders. The original idea came from the late Yale economist, and Nobel Laureate, James Tobin, in an effort to try to reduce the damaging effect which currency speculation has had on economies around the globe. Since the end of the Bretton Woods system of fixed exchange rates, currency transactions have grown at a much faster rate than international trade, foreign direct investment and tourism. Before the break-up of Bretton Woods, these three economic activities accounted for over 90 per cent of all currency transactions. In the 1990s, the share of currency transactions explained by international trade, foreign direct investment and tourism has fallen to around 10 per cent, meaning that around 90 per cent of currency transactions are speculative in nature (that is, the currency is purchased merely with the hope of its value going up, not to carry out a real economic activity). Such currency speculation has played an important contributory role in the financial crises of the 1990s, and it is felt that some system is needed to reduce the mobility of short-term capital, or at least to take out the profits in short-term speculation in small movements in currency values. As the chaos created by this speculative activity has very real impacts on those not participating in currency speculation, as anyone who lost their job during one of the many financial crisis of the 1990s will readily attest to, it can be seen as an externality and the Tobin Tax as an effort to include these costs in this activity.

A Tobin Tax is an excellent way in which some of the wealth of the new economy can be subject to taxation. However, any Tobin Tax system would need international cooperation and, although it has the potential to raise considerable amounts of money, given the high level of currency speculation (up to

$1.8 trillion per day), most proposals have earmarked the funds to go towards either environmental issues or towards development in the third world.

BIT TAX

Much of the new economy is based on the transmission of electronic information in the form of digital bits. Many of these exchanges, such as ATM transactions, e-mails, foreign exchange transfers, teleconferencing and electronic check clearance, are examples of the new economy doing business. All these activities exist because of a considerable level of public investment paid by taxpayers, and as they are now provided for the most part for free, you have the problem often associated with a free good — inefficient usage. A small tax on this traffic of information would promote a more efficient usage of these resources, and also provide a considerable amount of revenue that could go towards funding a Basic Income.

Our purpose in this book has been to show some of the effects that a Basic Income would have on the efficiency and equity of the Irish economy. In attempting to do this, we have simulated a Basic Income proposal that makes as few changes to the existing system as possible. In this chapter, we have looked at some of the possible ways our proposal can be modified. We have certainly not exhausted the variations that are possible, and if some time and energy were devoted to alternative funding systems, no doubt more creative means to fund a basic income could be developed.

Conclusion: Social Justice or Blind Drift?

> Every era of capitalist triumphalism creates the basis for renewed social struggle to ameliorate inequalities, a struggle to limit the new mechanisms of inequality. Every technological revolution has been accompanied by ruling elites calling for more flexibility (or whatever the word at the time) from workers and for more "discipline" over them. In such times, momentarily, the forward march of social progress seems to be halted, even revered. Then, once a vision of an alternative, viable system of distributive justice has crystallised, the state has moved in that direction, to re-embed the economy in society. Then — perhaps in directions that were not previously foreseen — the forward march resumes. (Guy Standing, quoted in Lerner, Clark and Needham, 1999, p. 106)

This book started off with a discussion on the values that should guide any discussion on Irish social policy. In this conclusion, we return to these criteria, using them as a score card to rate the competing approaches to how to promote economic progress and social justice; that is, ensuring future economic progress that all share in.

CORI Criteria

Our first set of criteria was those developed by the Conference of Religious of Ireland. These criteria have underpinned their extensive body of work on social policy issues. Our task now is to see how our proposed Basic Income system meets their stated specifications for tax and social welfare reform.

1. Nature and Its Resources are for the Benefit of All

A Basic Income system, by providing a universal income to all, necessarily benefits all. In fact, what our proposal does is take just under 17 per cent of GDP (€19.55 billion Basic Income costs plus social solidarity fund, divided by €115.55 billion GDP) and distribute it to all based on citizenship and age. Furthermore, as the economy grows, our proposal provides a mechanism to ensure that all share in the benefits of economic growth, in a manner that does not create barriers to future economic progress. Under the current system, the government is greatly limited in how it can help the poor and low paid. If it raises benefit levels, it creates poverty and unemployment traps. If it lowers taxes it merely helps the well-off, as the majority of poor and low-paid households do not benefit from tax cuts. The only other option is to intervene in the factor markets for labour and capital, which would destroy Ireland's competitive advantage in the new economy and the source of Ireland's recent economic growth.

2. Adequacy

Our proposed Basic Income system lifts all households above the 50 per cent median income poverty threshold. Under the current system, the ESRI projects increases in poverty rates, as the poorest 30 per cent of households have their share of aggregate income reduced (Nolan et al., 2000), even with the fastest-growing economy in the OECD.

3. Guaranteed

A Basic Income system is not means-tested and is thus guaranteed to all.

4. Eliminate Poverty Traps

Poverty traps under the current system exist due to the loss of benefit at a rate faster than after-tax earned income increases. As the Basic Income payment is not reduced by labour market participation or an increase in earned income, it does not cause poverty traps.

5. Equity

Under a Basic Income system, all people are treated the same, with the only difference in payments being determined by age. Our proposed Basic Income system has both vertical equity (households with the same number of members and earned incomes will pay the same tax and receive the same level of benefits) and it promotes horizontal equity as it creates a more equal distribution of income. The current system is generating greater income inequality.

6. Efficiency

In Chapters 4 and 5, we saw that a Basic Income system assists in the competitiveness of the economy, ensuring income security in a more flexible labour market environment. Under the current system, efforts to promote income security will require a reduction in competitiveness and flexibility.

7. Simplicity and Transparency

Any comparison between a Basic Income system and the existing systems of social welfare, in Ireland or anywhere else in the developed world, will clearly show that a Basic Income system is the simplest and most transparent option for providing income security.

8. Reduce Dependency

The elimination of means-testing and the provision of a universal payment system provides individuals with the independence to determine how best they can contribute to society through social participation. They will not be forced into idleness and long-term dependency. A Basic Income gives them the income independence that will allow them to achieve full autonomy.

GOALS OF THE NATIONAL ECONOMIC AND SOCIAL COUNCIL

1. Economic Inclusiveness through Full Employment

The employment benefits of a Basic Income system have long been noted. In Chapters 4 and 5, we have demonstrated that a Basic Income system promotes labour market participation and job creation. A Basic Income system allows for a more equitable sharing of employment and the benefits of economic progress, but more importantly, it allows for greater levels of all forms of social participation. Any policy that only promotes greater employment without taking into consideration other forms of social participation, the need to share the benefits of economic progress, and the need for the benefits of technological advancement to allow for more leisure for all, will merely create new forms of oppression. The logical conclusion to having full, paid employment as the only goal is to have every adult working 40-plus hours a week, including seniors. Thus, the net effect of this path of economic progress will be that everyone is working more and more. Add to this the loss in leisure and family time, the added stress of always rushing here to there, the increase in the commuting costs of traffic jams and congestion, and numerous other costs associated with consumerism, and the net effect of economic progress will be increased wealth for the few and a lower quality of life for everyone else. A Basic Income system promotes full participation; that is, real full employment — a job for everyone who wants paid employment — while at the same time supporting all those who wish to participate in the non-commercial aspects of society.

2. Adaptability, Full Development of Information Society, Lifelong Learning

One of the ways that a Basic Income system promotes labour market flexibility is through its support for people when they are out of the labour force. One of the reasons that we should expect there to be frequent periods of people being out of the labour force in the new economy is that they will have to periodically update their skills and receive more education and training. A Basic Income supports lifelong learning and allows the labour force to adapt itself to the changing structure of the labour market.

3. Sustainable and Balanced Regional Development

A Basic Income policy has been one of the key planks in the Green Party's platform since its inception for the simple reason that a Basic Income system is a necessary foundation to sustainable (environmental and social) development. A Basic Income system takes away the rationale of mindless growth in order to support the poor and unemployed. Everyone agrees that one cannot sacrifice the poor for the goal of reducing pollution, but the "rising tide lifts all boats" argument loses much of its appeal when the tide rises because of environmental or social pollution. We do not need a rising tide of market transactions that merely increase GDP but do not contribute to the well-being of the community (such as crime, pollution and family breakups). What is needed is a path of development that gives voice to human needs, regardless of the market power (and income) of the speaker. This a Basic Income system does in many ways. Furthermore, a Basic Income system will promote rural development, as the purchasing power of a Basic Income payment will be higher in the low-cost rural areas than in the higher cost urban areas. This increase in purchasing power in the rural areas will promote more economic activity in these regions and encourage people and businesses to relocate into these areas.

4. Further Development of the European Union

There is no doubt that Ireland has so far benefited greatly from its participation in the European Union, yet many further obstacles to a fully integrated European economy still exist. One of these is the radically different social welfare systems across Europe. Full monetary union will exacerbate these differences, and will force the issue of the need to harmonise these systems. Given that each respective system is the result of each country's particular history, it is unlikely that one country's current system will be able to meet the needs of all other countries. A Basic Income system will, however, allow for substantial harmonisation of social welfare systems across Europe while at the same time allowing for differences within countries reflecting their different costs of living, incomes and other factors, with the eventual goal of equalisation of payment rates and tax levels once income convergence has been achieved.

5. Entrepreneurial Culture

The great Institutionalist economist, C.E. Ayres, wrote that the institution of a universal guaranteed income "could . . . restore the reality of free private enterprise" (Ayres, 1965, p. 161). His argument is based partly on the positive aggregate demand effects such a system would have and partly on the great liberating effect economic security has on individuals. All societies attempt to provide some form of economic security. This is due to the simple fact that as individuals we are poor and that we only achieve affluence through the co-operation of others, i.e. life in society. Economic security allows for experimentation and knowledge creation. Communities that are living hand-to-mouth do not have the time or the resources to break out of poverty through technological or institutional change. The risk of failure is too great (starvation) for them to undertake such a gamble. The same is not true for individuals in an affluent society. Economic security provides the support for experimentation and risk-taking — what would be called in business circles entrepreneurship. A Basic Income thus supports an entrepreneurial culture, but it does so from the bottom up. There is no need to support entrepreneurship from the top down, since the profit motive does this adequately enough. To develop a culture of entrepreneurship will require starting at the bottom.

SUMMING UP

The debate on Basic Income in Ireland has gone through many stages (see Ward, 1998, for a history). When such policies were first proposed, they were met by the criticism that they were too expensive. The ESRI produced a report that suggested that such a policy would require tax rates of up to 67 per cent. Subsequent research has demonstrated that this is not the case, and the recent Working Group Report on Basic Income has finally settled the question: Ireland can afford a Basic Income (see http://www.irlgov.ie/taoiseach/publication/default.htm). A Basic Income can be implemented in Ireland with tax rates that are within the realm of Ireland's recent experience. The next set of objections to a Basic Income policy in Ireland state that it would kill the incentive for Irish men and women to seek paid employment. Clark and Kavanagh (1995) showed that this argument was both theoretically and empirically weak. In Chapter 5 of this book, we have further demonstrated that a Basic Income policy would have positive effects on the Irish labour market. Furthermore, we demonstrated that such a policy would support the competitiveness of the Irish economy, using the criteria of competitiveness adopted by the National Competitiveness Council. We have also shown that a Basic Income system will not only promote future economic progress, but will also help to ensure that all will share in this progress. Lastly, we have shown that a Basic Income system has the potential of lifting all households in Ireland out of material poverty.

The new economy is a reality that Ireland, and all other countries, has to face. It can face it by building on the positive aspects of technological change and globalisation in a way that ensures that all benefit from these developments, or it can just go along with the tide and allow those with power to determine the direction of the economy. The choice is between social justice, a society in which all benefit and all contribute, and a blind drift in a sea of market forces, concentrated economic power and falling quality of life. If Guy Standing, in the quotation that opens this conclusion, is correct, eventually some form of economic security system will be demanded by the people who are excluded from the new economy. It can happen through decades of social struggle or through making the rational and humane policy decisions now. But there is no denying that evolution in the economy will require an evolution in the institutions that provide economic security.

BIBLIOGRAPHY

Appelbaum, E. (1979), "The Labor Market" in *A Guide to Post Keynesian Economics*, edited by Alfred Eichner, New York: M.E. Sharpe.

Atkinson, A. (1995), *Public Economics in Action,* Oxford: Clarendon Press.

Ayres, C.E. (1966), "Guaranteed Income: An Institutionalist View" in *The Guaranteed Income: Next Step in Economic Evolution?* edited by R. Theobald, New York: Doubleday.

Barrett, A., T. Callan and B. Nolan (1999), "Rising wage inequality, returns to education and labour market institutions: Evidence from Ireland", *British Journal of Industrial Relations*, Vol. 37, No. 1, pp. 77–100.

Callan, T. and D. McCoy (eds.) (2001), *Budget Perspectives*, Dublin: ESRI.

Carnoy, M. (2000), *Sustaining the New Economy*, New York: Russell Sage.

Central Bank of Ireland (1997), *Quarterly Bulletin Autumn 1997*, Dublin: Central Bank of Ireland.

Central Bank of Ireland (2001), *Quarterly Bulletin Winter 2001*, Dublin: Central Bank of Ireland.

Central Statistics Office (1998), *National Income and Expenditure*, Dublin, Stationery Office.

Clark, C.M.A. (1998), "Unemployment in Ireland: A Post Keynesian Perspective" in *Unemployment in Ireland*, edited by C. Kavanagh and C.M.A. Clark, Aldershot, UK: Avebury.

Clark, C.M.A. and S. Healy (1997), *Pathways to a Basic Income*, Dublin: CORI.

Clark, C.M.A. and C. Kavanagh (1996a), "Basic Income, Inequality and Unemployment: Rethinking the Linkages between Work and Welfare" *Journal of Economic Issues*, June, Vol. 30, pp. 399–406.

Clark, C.M.A. and C. Kavanagh (1996b), "Progress, Values and Economic Indicators" in *Progress, Values and Public Policy*, edited by Brigid Reynolds and Sean Healy, Dublin: CORI.

Clark, J.M. (1923), *Studies in the Economics of Overhead Costs*, Chicago: University of Chicago Press.

Cobb, C., T. Halstead and J. Rowe (1995), "If the GDP is UP, Why is America Down?" *The Atlantic Monthly*, Vol. 276, October, pp. 59–78.

Collins, M. and C. Kavanagh (1998), "For Richer, For Poorer: The Changing Distribution of Household Income in Ireland, 1973–1994" in *Social Policy in Ireland*, edited by S. Healy and B. Reynolds, Dublin: Oak Tree Press.

Department of Finance (2000), *Budget 2000*, Dublin: Stationery Office.

Department of Finance (2001), *Budget 2001*, Dublin: Stationery Office.

Department of Social Welfare (1996), *Social Insurance in Ireland*, Dublin: Stationery Office.

Eatwell, J. (1995), "Disguised Unemployment: The G7 Experience" UNCTAD Discussion Paper.

Economic and Social Research Institute (1999), *Medium-Term Review 1999–2005*, Dublin: ESRI.

Bibliography

Expert Working Group on the Integration of the Tax and Social Welfare Systems (1996), *Report of the Expert Working Group on the Integration Tax and Social Welfare*, Dublin: Stationery Office.

Government of Ireland (1997), *National Anti-Poverty Strategy*, Dublin: Stationery Office.

Government of Ireland (1999), *1998 Statistical Information on Social Welfare Services,* Dublin: Stationery Office.

Healy, S. and B. Reynolds (1995), *Desirability, Viability, Impact*, Dublin: CORI.

Healy, S. and B. Reynolds (1999a), *Priorities for Progress*, Dublin: CORI.

Healy, S. and B. Reynolds (1999b), *Resources and Choices*, Dublin: CORI.

International Labor Organization (1999), *Key Indicators of the Labour Market*, Geneva: ILO.

Kennelly, B. and M. Collins (1999) "Social Exclusion and Social Partnership" in *Social Partnership in a New Century*, edited by B. Reynolds and S. Healy, Dublin: CORI.

Keynes, J.M. (1936), *The General Theory of Employment, Interest and Money*, London: Macmillan.

Keynes, John Maynard (1963), *Essays in Persuasion*, London: Macmillan.

Layte, R. et al. (2001), *Monitoring Poverty Trends and Exploring Poverty Dynamics in Ireland*, Dublin: ESRI.

Leoni, R. (1994), "Labour Supply: Which Theory: A Critical Empirical Assessment", *Labour* Vol. 8, No. 1, pp. 19–55.

Lerner, S., C.M.A. Clark, and W.R. Needham (1999), *Basic Income: Economic Security for All Canadians*, Toronto: Between the Lines.

McAleese, Dermot (1997), "Economic Policy and Performance: The Irish Experience", *Journal of the Statistical and Social Inquiry Society of Ireland*, Vol. XXVII, Part V, 1997/1998, pp 1–18.

McCarthy, D. (1999), "Building a Partnership", in *Social Partnership in a New Century*, edited by B. Reynolds and S. Healy, Dublin: CORI.

Marx, K. (1906), *Capital*, New York: The Modern Library.

Mitchell, B.R. (1992), *International Historical Statistics: Europe 1750-1988*, New York: Stockton Press.

National Competitiveness Council (2000), *Annual Competitiveness Report 2000*, Dublin: Forfás.

National Economic and Social Council (1999), *Opportunities, Challenges and Capacities for Choice*, Dublin: NESC.

Nolan, B., B. Maître, D. O'Neill and O. Sweetman (2000), *The Distribution of Income in Ireland*, Dublin: Oak Tree Press.

Nurmi, K. (1999), "Changes in Women's and Men's Labour Market Positions in the EU" in *Social Policy in Tandem with the Labour Market in the European Union*, Ministry of Social Affairs and Health, Finland. http://www.vn.fi/stm/english/tao/publicat/tandem/nurmi/kaarina.htm

O'Connell, P.J. (1999), "Astonishing success: Economic growth and the labour market in Ireland", Employment and Training Papers, 44, International Labour Organization.

O'Connor, C., E. O'Mara Walsh and C. Owens (1998), "Irish Outward Foreign Direct Investment: The Future Impetus for Economic Growth" *Student Economic Review*, Trinity College.

Organization of Economic Co-operation and Development (1999), *OECD Economic Outlook*, Paris: OECD.

Organization of Economic Cooperation and Development (2000), *OECD Economic Outlook*, Paris: OECD.

Organization of Economic Co-operation and Development (2001), *OECD Economic Outlook,* Paris: OECD.

Polanyi, K. (1944), *The Great Transformation*, Boston: Beacon Press.

Reynolds, B. and S. Healy (1994), *Towards an Adequate Income for All*, Dublin: CORI.

Reynolds, B. and S. Healy (1995), *An Adequate Income Guarantee for All,* Dublin: CORI.

Reynolds, B. and S. Healy (1996), *Progress, Values and Public Policy*, Dublin: CORI.

Reynolds, B. and S. Healy (1999), *Social Partnership in a New Century*, Dublin: CORI.

Ricardo, D. (1971) [1821], *Principles of Political Economy and Taxation*, New York: Dutton.

Rifkin, J. (1995), *The End of Work*, New York: G.P. Putnam and Sons.

Smith, A. (1976) [1776], *An Inquiry into the Nature and Causes of the Wealth of Nations*, Oxford: Oxford University Press.

Standing, G. (1999), *Global Labour Flexibility*, London: Macmillan Press Ltd.

Thurow, L. (1992), *Head to Head*, New York: Morrow.

Ward, S. (1998), "Basic Income" in *Social Policy in Ireland*, edited by S. Healy and B. Reynolds, Dublin: Oak Tree Press.

Wilkinson, R.G. (1996), *Unhealthy Societies: The Afflictions of Inequality*, London: Routledge.

Wolff, E. (1996), "Time for a Wealth Tax?" *Boston Review*, February/March. http://bostonreview.mit.edu/BR21.1/wolff.html